Jossey-Bass Teacher

Jossey-Bass Teacher provides educators with practical knowledge and tools to create a positive and lifelong impact on student learning. We offer classroom-tested and research-based teaching resources for a variety of grade levels and subject areas. Whether you are an aspiring, new, or veteran teacher, we want to help you make every teaching day your best.

From ready-to-use classroom activities to the latest teaching framework, our value-packed books provide insightful, practical, and comprehensive materials on the topics that matter most to K–12 teachers. We hope to become your trusted source for the best ideas from the most experienced and respected experts in the field.

PREVIOUS BOOKS BY MICHAEL GURIAN

PARENTING

Nurture the Nature

The Wonder of Children (previously published as *The Soul of the Child*)

The Wonder of Girls

The Wonder of Boys

A Fine Young Man

The Good Son

What Stories Does My Son Need? (with Terry Trueman)

PSYCHOLOGY

What Could He Be Thinking?

Love's Journey

Mothers, Sons and Lovers

The Prince and the King

EDUCATION

The Minds of Boys: Saving Our Sons from Falling Behind in School and Life (with Kathy Stevens)

Boys and Girls Learn Differently!: A Guide for Teachers and Parents (with Patricia Henley and Terry Trueman)

The Boys and Girls Learn Differently Action Guide for Teachers (with Arlette C. Ballew)

BUSINESS/CORPORATE

The Leading Partners Workbook (with Katherine Coles and Kathy Stevens)

FOR YOUNG ADULTS

Understanding Guys

From Boys to Men

FICTION AND POETRY

The Miracle

An American Mystic

The Odyssey of Telemachus

Emptying

As the Swans Gather

PREVIOUS BOOKS BY KATHY STEVENS

The Minds of Boys: Saving Our Sons from Falling Behind in School and Life (with Michael Gurian)

Leading Partners (with Michael Gurian and Katharine Coles)

Strategies for Teaching Boys and Girls— Elementary Level

A WORKBOOK FOR EDUCATORS

By Michael Gurian, Kathy Stevens, and Kelley King

JOSSEY-BASS
A Wiley Imprint
www.josseybass.com

Published by Jossey-Bass
A Wiley Imprint
989 Market Street, San Francisco, CA 94103–1741—www.josseybass.com

Readers should be aware that Internet Web sites offered as citations and/or sources for further information may have changed or disappeared between the time this was written and when it is read.

Jossey-Bass books and products are available through most bookstores. To contact Jossey-Bass directly call our Customer Care Department within the U.S. at 800–956–7739, outside the U.S. at 317–572–3986, or fax 317–572–4002.

Jossey-Bass also publishes its books in a variety of electronic formats. Some content that appears in print may not be available in electronic books.

ISBN: 978-07879-9730-4

Printed in the United States of America

FIRST EDITION

PB Printing   10 9 8 7 6 5 4 3 2 1

About This Book

S TRATEGIES *for Teaching Boys & Girls: A Workbook for Elementary Level Educators* is an invaluable resource for teachers working with students from preschool through fifth grade. It weaves together brain science and classroom strategies in a way that is both easily understandable and immediately applicable. This is the kind of book that teachers want—one that combines the right balance of "just enough" theory to help teachers become knowledgeable and a "whole bunch" of practice so that they can jump right in with the strategies on Monday morning.

We've organized this book around several important strategy domains so that you can go right to the sections that you need. We do suggest that you start with Chapter One to lay a foundation about the brain. After that, feel free to skip around to the parts you most need as a teacher. You'll find chapters on movement, visual teaching strategies, social interaction, offering choice, art and music integration, making learning relevant, and more. Each of these chapters provides a fascinating look at how the brain works and illuminates why these strategies are so important for all learners. Central to each chapter is an exploration of the differences between the male and female brain and the connection of these hard-wired differences to gender-specific teaching strategies. We think you'll appreciate the comments from students about their own learning, as well as the anecdotes from teachers about what works in the classroom.

The highlight of this book is the extensive lists of classroom activity and strategy ideas that span all content areas. We wanted to create a book for teachers that can be read and re-read many times over and that will be a source of creativity and inspiration for years to come. We hope that our ideas may infuse a new level of excitement, curiosity, and student learning in your classroom.

The Authors

Michael Gurian is a social philosopher, family therapist, corporate consultant, and the *New York Times* bestselling author of twenty books published in twenty-one languages. The Gurian Institute, which he co-founded, conducts research internationally, launches pilot programs, and trains professionals.

As a social philosopher, Michael has pioneered efforts to bring neurobiology and brain research into homes, workplaces, schools, and public policy. A number of his groundbreaking books in child development, including *The Wonder of Boys, Boys and Girls Learn Differently!, The Wonder of Girls,* and *What Could He Be Thinking?,* as well as *The Minds of Boys* (coauthored with Kathy Stevens), have sparked national debate. His newest work, *Nurture the Nature* (2007), provides a revolutionary new framework, based in neurobiology, by which to understand and care for children all the way from birth to adulthood.

A former university instructor, Michael has worked as a consultant to school districts, families, therapists, community agencies, and other organizations. He keynotes regularly at conferences and has lectured at such leading institutions as Harvard University, Johns Hopkins University, Stanford University, and UCLA. His training videos are used by Big Brother and Big Sister agencies throughout North America.

Michael's work has been featured in various media, including *The New York Times,* the *Washington Post, USA Today, Newsweek, Time, Educational Leadership, Parenting, Good Housekeeping, Redbook,* and on the *Today Show, Good Morning America,* CNN, PBS and National Public Radio.

Kathy Stevens, executive director of the Gurian Institute, is an international presenter and coauthor of *The Minds of Boys.* Her work has been featured in national publications including *Newsweek, Reader's Digest, Educational Leadership, Education Week, National School Board Journal,* and *Library Journal.*

Kathy has over twenty-five years of experience working in the nonprofit sector, focusing on children, youth, families, and women's issues. Her professional experience includes teaching music in Pre-K–8, designing and administering programs in early childhood care and education, domestic violence, juvenile corrections, adult community corrections, teen pregnancy prevention, cultural competency, and women's issues. Much of her early work was done in economically disadvantaged minority communities.

In addition to her work with the Gurian Institute, Kathy has designed and delivered training for the Federal Bureau of Prisons, Virginia Department of Corrections, Girl Scouts, U.S. Navy Ombudsman Program, Disproportionate Minority Confinement Task Force and a variety of nonprofit organizations. As a diversity trainer, she was honored to participate in the Children's Defense Fund's Institute for Cultural Competency at the former Alex Haley Farm in Tennessee.

Kathy lives in Colorado Springs with her husband. She has two sons and seven grandchildren.

Kelley King, director of the Gurian Institute's education division, has been a classroom teacher, special education teacher, teacher of the gifted, and a school administrator for twenty years.

While a school principal, Kelley initiated and led her school through an improvement process targeted at closing the gender gap, including the analysis of the data, professional dialogue and training, and the identification and implementation of effective strategies. Through action research, she has been able to demonstrate the effectiveness of *The Minds of Boys* and *Boys and Girls Learn Differently!* theory to enhance the achievement of all students.

Through her work with the Gurian Institute, Kelley presents at schools and conferences across the United States. Her work has been featured in national publications including *Newsweek* and *Educational Leadership,* and she is regularly interviewed by local and national media.

Kelley and her husband, Chris, live in Superior, CO with their two children.

About the Gurian Institute

IF you would like to help your school and community better understand how gender affects learning and living, please contact the Gurian Institute. Through our four divisions—Education, Family, Human Services, and Corporate—we provide training and services to schools, school districts, institutions of higher education, parent groups, businesses, youth-serving organizations, juvenile and adult corrections, medical and mental health professionals, religious organizations, and others serving boys and girls, and men and women.

We also provide keynotes and breakouts at conferences worldwide. There are Gurian Institute trainers throughout the United States, and in Canada, Australia, China and France.

We are committed to helping school districts, corporations and agencies become self-sufficient through internal training-of-trainer models. These are ongoing and serve populations over the long term.

A highlight of our training year is our annual Summer Training Institute, in Colorado Springs. Professionals join together for four days of training and networking. Some individuals become certified on the fifth day.

The Institute also provides books, workbooks, training videos for educators and parents, newsletters for parents and teachers, online courses and live chats, as well as other products.

For more information on services, products, and our philosophy, please visit www.gurianinstitute.com.

GURIAN INSTITUTE

Acknowledgments

TEACHING is both a craft and an art. Each new teacher arrives in the classroom with a toolbox filled with ideas, strategies, passions, and hopes that will be transformed into opportunities for children, boys and girls, to learn how to read, add, subtract, think, ponder, and dream. With every passing school year teachers add new tools to their toolbox—they learn from professional development opportunities, from each other, from mentors, and they learn from the children.

The Gurian Institute has been invited into classrooms around the country, meeting wonderful educators who have honored us by allowing us to help them expand their toolbox. They have been the motivation and inspiration for this book. Dedicated administrators and teachers are working every day to understand how boys and girls learn differently, and by so doing help every student reach as high as she or he can. This book is richer as a result of teachers sharing their successes and students adding their voices. We are grateful to each and every one of them. We especially must acknowledge:

- Our Gurian Institute certified trainers, whose expertise and dedication carries them to hundreds of schools every year, sharing their knowledge and experience with their colleagues, practicing what they preach, improving the odds for each boy and girl who enters a classroom. Many of our trainers are educators just like you—principals, classroom teachers, curriculum specialists, school counselors—working in schools rich in diversity, challenge, and success.

- The outstanding educators in the Boulder Valley School District, especially Ellen, an exceptional mentor and role-model, and the magnificent teachers and staff of Douglass Elementary School.

- All the schools, teachers, administrators, and students who shared their wisdom and feelings with us—they make the book more real.

- The professionals who took time in their already over-booked lives to review the manuscript and offer invaluable feedback.

- The editorial staff at Jossey-Bass is simply the best in the business! The wisdom and support of Lesley Iura, Julia Parmer, Margie McAneny, Natalie Lin, Kate Gagnon, Pam Berkman, Dimi Berkner, and, as always, Alan Rinzler have combined to make it truly a better book than it would have been without their help.

Dedication

Michael: For Gail, Gabrielle, and Davita, and all the teachers.

Kathy: To all the teachers who dedicate themselves daily to offer each girl and boy a chance to develop to her or his fullest potential. I am in awe!

Kelley: I could not have participated in writing this book without the patience, understanding and support of my family. My husband, Chris, coached me to take it one step at a time as I pondered the magnitude of writing a book on top of being a full-time school principal. My children, Connor and Roxanne, were always so understanding when I sequestered myself in the study for long periods of time. They have been my greatest teachers about gender differences—as evidenced by my son's exasperated inquiry one night, "Why do you have to write a book? That just means that people like me have to read it."

Contents

The Science of Boy-Girl Learning Differences

1

A primary concern for nearly every teacher is the difference we each intuit in the males and females we teach. We all know that there is immense overlap between the genders, and that each child is an inherently sacrosanct individual not to be limited by a gender stereotype, but we also know that boys and girls learn differently right before our eyes.

—Michael Gurian

IN the past couple of decades one question has taken on more and more significance when we consider how ready an individual child might be for entering school: Is the child a boy or a girl? Exciting and ongoing research into the living brains of boys and girls is showing us that not only are boys and girls different at the organic level, but how they learn is different in many, many ways from the day they are born.

In the early days of the Gurian Institute's work with educators, we would ask the question, "How many of you took a course on how boys and girls learn differently during your teacher training in college?" Even in audiences of several hundred teachers, no hands would go up. When we ask that same question today, a few hands might go up. When questioned further, those who raise their hands generally report that they covered the topic of gender and learning briefly in an education class.

At the same time, when teachers take our course in how boys and girls learn differently they often ask, "Why isn't this taught in college? Why aren't schools of education teaching this?" Fortunately, more and more are every day. Many are catching up to the newest brain research in learning, development, and gender.

The book you are about to read is based on twenty years of in-school research and ten years of training teachers in the practical strategies that grow from teaching (and learning) that work. You'll meet many teachers in this book, and your toolbox will be increased manifold.

You'll also have a head start on the education course that will, we hope, be taught in every school of education in the future.

Boys and Girls Learn Differently!

This chapter will give you an overview of the latest information available on how boys and girls learn differently and how that difference can and should change the way you implement your curriculum to ensure that every child, male and female, will have the chance to succeed to his or her maximum potential. For many of you, this information will bring an "Aha!" that validates intuitions you've had for a long time. We hope it will confirm that you have been on the right path as you work with your students. We hope that, for many of you, this information will open the door to exciting new experiences as you implement what you learn.

Where and when does gender in the brain begin? Soon after conception, boys and girls are on diverging development paths. If a child receives an X chromosome from each parent, a female architectural plan goes into action. If a child received one X chromosome and one Y chromosome, a different plan is activated and a male system is designed. These plans result in not only different bodies, but different brains. Beginning at around six weeks, a male fetus triggers biological mechanisms toward the secretion of large amounts of testosterone in his fetal system. His genitals drop, producing the testosterone he needs. From that point until somewhere between five and six months of development, testosterone becomes the "chief engineer" of the developing male's body and brain, giving him the capacity for a higher muscle mass than a female, different iron and calcium ratios, and different brain "formatting." Developing female fetuses receive testosterone during the developmental period between six weeks and six months in utero, but not as much. They receive more estrogen-type hormones. This helps format their brains to be female. By six months in utero, boys and girls have been formatted with different brains.

Are these differences all that matter? Of course not. There are many similarities between girls and boys in utero and once they are born. There are also many differences among girls and among boys that indicate how powerfully individual personalities can trump gender in importance. Furthermore, the way a child is nurtured can affect how he manifests his maleness and she her femaleness.

Caveats aside, gender is a big deal—especially in learning. One can make the argument, if one wished to, that every boy could cry as much as every girl, or that every boy could talk about his feelings as much as every girl (it would be a tough argument, but social theories can make it); however, the brain research on gender difference is now so detailed, it is no longer possible to responsibly argue that boys and girls learn the same way.

What *Are* the Differences?

Although researchers are still discovering new areas of difference between the male and female brain, a number have already been identified that have implications for how boys and girls learn. Remember that we are generalizing based on relevant research. There will be exceptions to each generalization, as every child is an individual, and male and female brain difference ranges both between boys and girls and among boys and girls. Remember also that difference means only that—one is not better than the other. Both are equally capable of learning and succeeding, but they do so in ways that we must understand if we are to create an educational environment that meets the needs of both!

Structural Differences

Using *magnetic resonance imaging* (MRI), *positron emission tomography* (PET) and *single photon emission computed tomography* (SPECT) technologies, scientists can look at the living brain and watch it work. The most advanced technologies let researchers watch actual blood flow in the brain, see where the brain is working, and by looking at male and female brains in this way, can see that boys and girls are working in different areas when completing the same tasks.

Over the past couple of decades, technology has helped researchers focus on some specific areas of structural difference between the male and female brain. Following are some of the most significant differences and their potential impact on your classroom.

Corpus Callosum—This dense bundle of nerves connects the two hemispheres of the brain. In females, this bundle of nerves tends to be denser and larger than in males, resulting in increased cross-talk between the left and right hemispheres. The anterior commisure, a tiny additional connection between the unconscious areas of the hemispheres attached to the end of the corpus callosum, is also larger in females.

> *And this means*—girls are generally better at multitasking than boys, including watching and listening and making notes at the same time. It also may explain why girls tend to tune into their own and others' feelings and move emotional content more quickly into thought and verbal processes. Girls can tell you how they feel as they are feeling—boys often need time to process before they can explain feelings.

Brain Stem—This is the most primitive part of our brain. Our "fight or flight" responses come from the brain stem; when we're threatened or in crisis this area of our brain takes over, telling the body how to respond.

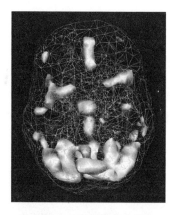

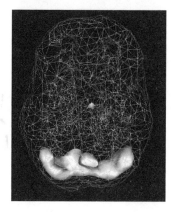

Amen Scans of the Female Brain (top) and Male Brain (bottom) at rest. The areas you see that look like bubbles are areas of activity— while at rest!

SPECT scans used by permission of Dr. Daniel Amen

With the male brain's greater amount of spinal fluid, messages tend to move more quickly from the brain to the body.

> *And this means*—boys' brains tend to be poised for fight or flight and for a physical response when they feel threatened or emotionally charged. Boys in your class may slam a book, kick a chair, use an expletive, or engage in some other kind of physical display when challenged. This behavior may be the result of an emotionally charged incident when the boy is not given enough time to process the emotional content.

Limbic System—This system is a collection of structures located under the corpus callosum and just above the brain stem, most of which are duplicated in each hemisphere of the brain. Within the limbic system are several structures that play a key role in how boys and girls learn and perform differently. Parts of the limbic system that process emotion and sensorial memory are, in general, more active in girls than in boys, resulting in increased emotional memory for females. Additionally, females tend to be better able to read emotional cues in others.

- *Hippocampus.* A key player in converting information from working memory into long-term or permanent memory. This process is crucial for learning to have meaning and for retention. The hippocampus tends to be larger in females and the speed of neural transmissions is faster than in males, resulting in generally increased memory storage for the female brain.

- *Amygdala.* A small, almond-shaped structure connected to one end of the hippocampus that plays a very important role in the processing of emotions, especially fear and anger. The amygdala tends to be larger in males. Some researchers believe that the close proximity of the amygdala to the hippocampus suggests that emotional content is "tagged" onto many long-term memories. Consequently, recalling a memory can recall an emotion as well.

> *And this means*—boys often display increased aggressive or impulsive responses—they tend to be sent to the principal a lot more than girls! Girls attach more emotional and sensory detail to events and remember them longer. They can hold grudges a long time. Writing stories will tend, on average, to be easier for girls when words are the only medium of inspiration used to help set up the paper.

Cerebral Cortex—This part of the brain contains about ten thousand miles of neural connections in each cubic inch! As thick as about three of your hairs, this area is where the serious intellectual functions of the brain take place. Thinking, speaking, and recalling—all things that need to happen in a classroom—are controlled in the cerebral cortex. The female brain tends to have more connections between neurons in the cerebral cortex. Blood flow in the brain is up to 20 percent greater in the female brain. Along with the increased neural connectivity between hemispheres, this adds more potential for information to move quickly between areas of the brain.

> *And this means*—the increased speed of their neural connections may help girls process and respond to classroom information faster than boys, help them make transitions faster, help them multitask, and help them access needed verbal resources (reading, writing, complex speech early in life) better than the average boy as they engage in learning.

Cerebellum—This is the "doing center" of the brain. It is larger in the male. Coupled with about 15 percent more spinal fluid in the male neural system, messages between the brain and body can move more quickly (and with less impulse control) in the male body.

> *And this means*—boys often learn better when their bodies are in motion. Sitting still can frustrate the male system, causing him to exhibit behavior that can appear disruptive or impulsive, and sometimes land him in the principal's office because he "can't sit still, can't stop touching things, is distracting his classmates" when he's really responding to his biological needs.

Processing Differences

Studying the images of the working brain, researchers find that not only are there structural differences between the brains of males and females, but there are also differences in how they use their brains. This has significance for teachers, as you develop strategies to implement your curriculum in ways that will allow all your students, both boys and girls, to perform at their best.

Here are just a few of the processing differences that have the most impact on learning.

Language Processing Areas—These areas are different in the male and female brain. Whereas males tend to have these areas centralized in the left hemisphere, females have multiple language processing areas in both hemispheres. As a result, females have more access to verbal resources than males, and therefore develop language earlier.

> *And this means*—girls generally have significantly more access to verbal resources when they start school, and throughout life, than boys. On average, females use twice the number of words that males do (this includes writing and reading). It is easier for them to learn to read and write in kindergarten and first grade. Because literacy is the foundation

of learning, this early difference often results in gender gaps that show up early in elementary school and persist throughout middle and high school.

Spatial Processing Areas—These areas are also significantly different in the male and female brain. Testosterone, the primary architect of the male brain, is believed to create more and denser neural connections in the right hemisphere of the male brain, with the result that males have increased resources for spatial reasoning—mental manipulation of objects, gross motor skills, mathematical reasoning, abstract reasoning, and the like. With less testosterone at work during fetal development, females tend to have less right hemisphere area devoted to spatial resources. (A crucial note: although girls generally test out worse than boys in spatial manipulation tests, there is less of a gender gap in mathematical calculation. Girls are not worse at math, as has been the stereotype in the past).

And this means—boys tend to need more space in which to function while they are learning, need to move more during learning, and are generally more interested in and often better at spatial tasks than girls. This shows up more in science and technology classes (a crucial area for those of us teaching girls and working toward parity). Girls will often find it easier to sit still and be quiet at their desks while doing seat work, but they may not gravitate as quickly to computers. They may need extra encouragement for this.

Sensory Systems—Females tend to process more data across the senses. Girls generally see better (in certain kinds of light), hear better, have a better sense of smell, and take in more information tactilely.

And this means—girls will be likely to include more sensory detail in their writing and conversation. They will generally use more varied color in their artwork. Boys will often use less sensory descriptors in their writing, an area in which those of us working with boys must be quite vigilant. Boys may also have a more difficult time hearing certain ranges of sound, especially from their usual, self-selected seat in the back of the room!

Chemical Differences

Male and female bodies are chemical plants! Hormones, neurotransmitters, all variety of proteins, nutrients—on the molecular level there is chemistry happening in every one of our cells all the time. And there are differences in the male and female laboratories. There are differences in the types and amounts of hormones and neurotransmitters that affect how boys and girls learn and interact. We've mentioned some of these. Let's now look more closely at them.

Testosterone—Testosterone is the male sex and aggression hormone, responsible for the architecture of the male system before birth, and for increased male aggression, competitiveness, self-assertion, and self-reliance throughout life. Male testosterone levels rise when males "win" and decline when males "lose." Female testosterone levels, always lower than males, remain basically constant and are not as subject to fluctuations brought about by winning or losing.

> *And this means*—healthy competition in the classroom will help motivate boys. Research has shown that boys tend to score better on tests at times when testosterone levels are high, and levels rise during competition. Using games that provide all students a chance to succeed, even if they are competing against themselves and "beating themselves" at a task, can be very productive. And although girls' testosterone levels don't fluctuate as boys' do, research shows that they gain self-confidence from active, healthy competition.

Estrogen—Estrogen is not one hormone, but a group of hormones, identified as the female sex hormone. Estrogens are present in both males and females, but they are usually present at significantly higher levels in girls and women, and promote the development of female secondary sex characteristics. Researchers have found that estrogen levels may affect aggressive tendencies in females, and levels may be affected by seasonal variations, such as length of daylight hours. Additionally, girls with increased amounts of body fat may be subject to earlier onset of puberty, as the body believes it is more prepared for reproduction because of increased hormone levels.

> *And this means*—for elementary girls who are overweight, puberty may be coming earlier and earlier, bringing with it increased levels of estrogen and the potential for more volatile mood swings and more aggressive behavior. When outward signs of puberty become noticeable, the brain changes that accompany puberty are also beginning. These changes can have a significant impact on behavior and performance for girls, beginning as early as third or fourth grade.

Serotonin—Serotonin is a neurotransmitter known as the "feel good" chemical. It affects mood, anxiety, and helps us to relax and cool off during times of conflict. Girls' levels of serotonin tend to be about 30 percent higher, making them less apt to rely on a fight response when in a conflict. Dr. Bruce Perry has studied neurotransmitters and found them to be responsive to environmental stimuli and reports that "kindness can be physically calming," helping to increase serotonin levels. Once angered, boys have less access to serotonin to help them manage their anger.

> *And this means*—boys will have less serotonin in their system to help them calm down and to de-escalate volatile situations. A calm, kind, supportive adult intervention will be more helpful than an adult who engages in a power struggle, escalating the boy's fight response.

Dopamine—Dopamine is a neurotransmitter that stimulates motivation and pleasure circuits in the brain of both boys and girls. Dopamine is critical to the way the brain controls our movements. Not enough dopamine? We can't move or control our movements well. Too much dopamine? Uncontrollable or subconscious movements (such as picking, tapping, repetitive moments, jerking, twitching) are observable. Dopamine also controls the flow of information between areas of the brain, especially memory, attention and problem-solving tasks.

> *And this means*—once boys are "revved up" with dopamine, their lower levels of serotonin will make it harder for them to come down. Their increased stimulation may actually tend to stimulate them more, causing them to spiral more and more out of control. A balance must be found in the classroom to help students get a "dopamine rush" from learning, but in an environment that provides enough structure to manage enthusiasm.

Oxytocin—Oxytocin is often referred to as the "tend and befriend" hormone, and is related to social recognition and bonding. Researchers have shown that oxytocin is involved in the formation of trust between people, and females have significantly higher levels in their systems than males throughout life. Oxytocin promotes the development and maintenance of relationships and females are biologically driven to maintain relationships, even those that are sometimes best let go.

> *And this means*—girls will be motivated by their chemical system to establish and maintain relationships with teachers and peers, and will behave in ways meant to meet that need, including pleasing the teacher. Boys are less chemically driven to establish and maintain these relationships prima facie, and may not see their behavior as having as much direct connection to their relationship with the teacher and their peers.

The Two Hemispheres

Hormones, processing, and structural elements exist throughout the brain, and especially in the two hemispheres. Quite interestingly—and this has an impact on learning—the male and female brains "do" their hemispheres somewhat differently.

Left-hemisphere preference is more common in *girls.* The left brain

- Is connected to the right side of the body
- Processes information sequentially and analytically
- Generates spoken language
- Recognizes words and numbers, when the numbers are spoken as words
- Responds more sensually to external stimuli
- Constructs memories (including hyperbolic memories)
- Does arithmetic functions
- Seeks explanations for occurrence of events

Right-hemisphere preference is more common in *boys.* The right brain

- Is connected to the left side of the body
- Processes information abstractly and holistically
- Interprets language non-verbally
- Recognizes places, faces, objects, music
- Fantasizes abstractions (such as science fiction and video game scenarios)
- Is less detailed and more concrete in recall
- Does relational and mathematical functions
- Organizes occurrences into spatial patterns

Male and female brains function in both hemispheres, but the right- and left-hemisphere preference of boys and girls has important implications when we look at how our schools are designed. Most educators will admit that schools are designed to be more left-hemisphere friendly: they are structured environments with time periods and ringing bells, are organized based on facts and rules, rely primarily on verbal processing, limit access to free space and movement, and require lots of multitasking.

Because this left-hemisphere-friendly environment naturally favors left-hemisphere preferences, girls are going to find school, in general, more comfortable than will many boys. Not surprisingly, schools report that 80 to 90 percent of their discipline problems are created by boys. Boys are not only biochemically more prone to "make a fuss" than girls but also quite often chafing against an environment that doesn't fit their right-hemisphere preference as learners.

If you would like a more comprehensive overview of the differences between the male and female brain, you might want to read *Boys and Girls*

Learn Differently! and *The Wonder of Girls* (by Michael Gurian) and *The Minds of Boys* (by Michael Gurian and Kathy Stevens).

Looking at the Male-Female Brain Spectrum

Male and female brains are different, but it's important to remember that one male brain is also different from another male brain; the same is true of female brains. All of us, male and female, fall somewhere on the male-female brain spectrum, a continuum from "the most male" to "the most female." Some boys' brains are more like the average girl's, and some girls' brains are more like the average boy's. What do we mean by that?

Researchers have identified what Michael Gurian labels "bridge brains," brains that fall in the middle of that spectrum. These are brains that are wired for more male and female brain architecture overlap. Research conducted by the Amen Clinics (which have performed thirty-five thousand brain scans) in the United States, and research by Professor Simon Baron-Cohen at Cambridge in the United Kingdom has confirmed the wide spectrum of male and female brains, as well as the existence of males and females very much in the middle of that spectrum. According to Baron-Cohen's scans, for instance, approximately one in five women and one in seven men are believed to fall within the bridge-brain range. These bridge brains are most easily seen after puberty.

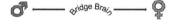

A female bridge brain might have a brain system inclined to process more like a male brain. Women who enjoy careers that are very competitive and highly spatial, and that require a higher degree of risk-tolerance—such as criminal law or engineering—might likely be bridge brains. A male bridge brain might be a man who enjoys a career requiring more verbal and emotional sensitivity and processing—such as a male kindergarten teacher.

Although bridge brains are not as easily identified in elementary school, it's important to be on the lookout for children who might think just a little differently from others of their gender. Providing a diverse array of ways to learn meets the needs of children who don't fit any generalization and validates that who they are is just great!

Gender Difference: A Path to Success

Understanding that boys' and girls' brains are wired differently is just the beginning. Focusing on how those differences impact the classroom is the next step. This workbook focuses on how you can you design strategies to meet the needs of boys and girls in your elementary classrooms.

The Gurian Institute Training Division has worked in more than a thousand schools throughout the United States and Canada, public and private, coed and single-sex. This work has been utilized in classrooms by over twenty-five thousand teachers in the United States, Canada, and Australia.

By helping teachers, administrators, parents, and others working with children to understand the differences in how boys and girls learn, and by providing (and gathering from wise teachers) strategies that work, schools are changing the way they do the business of education. They are succeeding in closing achievement gaps, helping at-risk students, helping students with learning disabilities, and creating classroom stability.

Schools and teachers who use the strategies suggested in this book have provided us with success data in these quantitative areas:

- Test scores
- Grades
- Discipline referrals

The strategies and best practices in this workbook have been field tested and provide a toolbox that can help you increase test scores and grades, and lower discipline referrals. We have gathered for you a number of Web sites, resources, and in-class projects and tools that you can begin to use today. Our recommendations work for both boys and girls—hindering neither. Many of these strategies and practices grow from research and from teachers' wisdom of practice that target boys or girls specifically, but we have not included (and never support) a practice that would be detrimental to either boys or girls.

This is one example of the success that can occur when teachers and schools understand how boys and girls learn differently, and when schools provide training and resources to help teachers implement effective strategies. Every teacher at Douglass knows that one strategic approach is not the only cause of statistical gains in test scores. Teachers can try many things, and many variables can affect improved learning. At the same time, Douglass teachers were happy to see rewards for their focus on how boys and girls learn differently. By visiting the Gurian Institute Web site (www.gurianinstitute.com) you can read more success stories and learn more about how teachers and schools are improving performance and helping kids excel.

Now we hope you'll enjoy the remaining chapters of this book, which show you how to implement strategies like those at Douglass in your own elementary classroom right now. We hope, too, that what you read here will resonate with your life experience as a teacher and make you say, perhaps a little more often than you did before, "I sure love teaching these kids."

Douglass Elementary: A Success Story

Kelley King, coauthor of this workbook, was principal of Douglass Elementary School in Boulder, Colorado when she met Michael Gurian and Kathy Stevens. Her school is a success story in applying strategies for teaching boys and girls specifically. Douglass has been featured in *Educational Leadership,* the *American School Board Journal,* in *Newsweek,* and even on the *Today Show.*

In August 2004, Douglass faculty studied their achievement data and noted a gap in achievement between boys and girls in writing. Having developed programming to address math and science gaps among girls, Douglass now noticed a significant gap for boys in reading and writing. The Douglass faculty, under the guidance of Kelley and the gender team, decided to establish a school improvement goal to close the gap through the implementation of instructional strategies shown to be effective in accommodating the brain differences of boys while meeting the needs of girls.

The teachers and principal studied the research in Michael Gurian's book, *Boys and Girls Learn Differently!* and an article by Michael Gurian and Kathy Stevens titled "With Boys and Girls in Mind," from *Educational Leadership.* The instructional strategies recommended by Michael and Kathy included the following:

- Increasing movement and kinesthetic learning opportunities

- Expanding the selection of reading materials to interest boys and girls specifically in classrooms

- Teaching and encouraging visual-spatial representations of thinking, especially during the planning stages of writing

- Creating a greater sense of purpose by offering expanded audiences for writing, thus helping shy students, among them many girls, to find voice, and helping many unmotivated boys to see the power of their work on an audience

- Creating a greater sense of relevancy across the curriculum through more student choice of topics in writing

- Increasing the participation of male role models in reading and writing in classrooms

- Offering some opportunities for single-sex activities within a classroom (such as all-boy and all-girl literature circles)

- Offering real-life simulations, such as reenactments and debates, to engage boys emotionally, and stimulate girls toward greater real-world learning

After the first year of implementation of these and other strategies, Douglass saw quantitative results in their writing achievement scores—especially for boys, but also for all sub-groups of students. For example, the overall gap between boys' and girls' performance in writing decreased from 13 percentage points to 5 percentage points, which was the target goal. This broke a cycle of girls outperforming boys by 13 to 16 percentage points over the prior three years. Not only did more boys reach proficiency, but more boys also reached the advanced levels or proficiency. Weighted index scores provide a clearer picture of student performance across all levels of proficiency. When examined as weighted index score gains and broken down by grade level, boys in third grade made a 7 point jump. Boys in fourth grade jumped from a weighted index score of 92 in third grade to 96 in fourth grade. An increase jump from 93 to 106—a full 13 points—was made by students in fifth grade.

A parent on the Douglass Elementary School Improvement team put these numbers in perspective. She said, "My son started the year in tears about writing. You folks did all these things and the change was almost immediate. Now, at the end of the year, he loves writing." This mom's comments reveal not only the improvement in achievement, but also a crucial element of success that Douglass focused on: parent buy-in and involvement.

In June 2006, Douglass Elementary School completed its second year of implementing gender-friendly instructional strategies in all classrooms. In addition to ongoing professional reading, Douglass Elementary School and a number of other Boulder Valley schools hosted the Gurian Institute for a full day of teacher training. Whereas the gender gap had been reduced to 4 percentage points after year one of implementation, after year two, the gap was reduced to a statistically insignificant 3 percentage points. There now is, statistically, no achievement gap in reading between boys and girls at Douglass.

A further gain has occurred among special education students. Because three out of four special needs students at Douglass were boys, Kelley and her staff suspected that meeting the gender-specific needs of boys would have a great impact on the special education population. In fact, in the two years of implementation, Douglass special needs students made substantially greater and more rapid gains than the special needs students in the school district as a whole. Currently, Douglass special education students are scoring almost 50 weighted index score points above the district average for this subgroup of students.

Douglass is seeing similar positive benefits in the area of math. There is no gender gap in either math or science now. As with literacy, these gains have occurred not just among general student populations, but also among special education students. Their math scores increased by 31 percentage points, with

Douglass students out-performing district special education students by 75 percentage points.

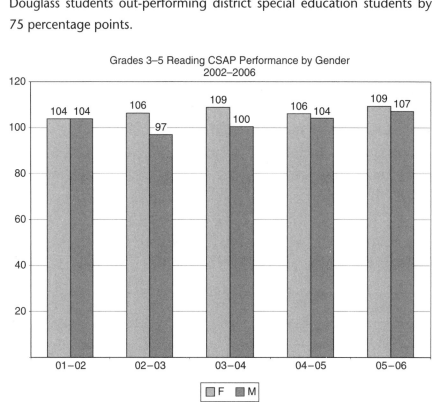

Grades 3–5 Reading CSAP Performance by Gender
2002–2006

In year three of implementation, Douglass teachers are becoming increasingly skilled in developing, using, and refining instructional tools in their classrooms that engage both boys and girls, and that honor, challenge, and build on the unique strengths that boys bring to the classroom setting.

Keep 'Em Moving

2

Incorporating Movement Across the Curriculum

Movement is about living, and living is about learning.

—Eric Jensen

THE bodies of children were not designed for sitting in a chair six hours a day. They were built for running, walking, crouching, squatting, touching. They were designed, especially in the elementary school years, to discover the world by moving around within it, bouncing against it, feeling themselves a part of it. Movement is extremely important to help both boys and girls learn, but can be especially urgent for many boys in a given classroom.

In today's classrooms, sitting is, unfortunately, the "activity" students are told to do the most. Oftentimes, we teachers "teach to the students' heads" and forget about everything from the shoulders down. Under tremendous pressure to cover more content in less time—with high-stakes testing just around the corner every year—it's natural for us to gravitate to what might seem like a "faster" means of imparting content. And sitting down isn't necessarily a bad thing. Reading, writing, listening, memorizing . . . all can happen while sitting.

But some things just can't happen. Some things can't be learned. Some children can't learn well without becoming a part of the learning process through movement. Many of these children are boys. Their bodies and brains are not wired to sit still as much as we might wish.

One wonderful development over the last two decades is the plethora of brain-based information available that supports the merits of letting kids move around as they learn. The key finding of this research can be summarized in one statement: grades and test scores will improve and discipline referrals to the principal will decrease when physical activity is integrated helpfully into a child's educational day. With the majority of

? DID YOU KNOW? Learning Loves Movement!

Cells and chemicals throughout the body are stimulated when the body moves. This stimulation improves learning because learning that is paired with movement often anchors better in the procedural memory centers of the brain. The increased blood flow and oxygen to the brain, along with the release of neurotransmitters, help students to learn concepts and procedures better and to retain them longer. When the body is helping the brain to learn, the brain is less likely to forget what's been learned.

Movement can be important for all children, but boys' brains generally need more movement than girls' in order to learn the same material. This is true for boys (and very active girls) not only because of improvements in procedural memory, but also because of impulse-control improvement. For many young males, learning is impeded by discipline problems associated with their own lack of impulse control. "Sit still!" the teacher will cry, just hoping the boy will stop fidgeting. Allowing the kind of physical movement that we'll explore in this chapter actually stimulates the young boy's brain while helping him to self-manage impulsive behavior. Movement has to be guided by teachers with authority, of course, and in effective, not distracting ways.

discipline referrals falling on boys, adding more movement to learning can dramatically reduce the number of boys in line at the principal's office.

What's our first clue that we might need to do more in our classes with physical movement? It will most probably appear in the behavior of our students. If we see five or more of them fidgeting, zoning out, missing out on directions (because they are zoning out), and even getting into trouble, we probably have not integrated enough physical movement into their learning.

Brain-Body Connections for Learning

First-grade teacher Sophie Trujillo-Schrock incorporates movement every day across her curriculum. "I greet the students with music playing," she reports. "The music I choose to play depends on the unit of study. The music plays while students unpack their backpacks, sign in for lunch, and they move to the beat all the way to our meeting area on the floor. Currently, I'm playing a lot of jazz and Mardi Gras music because we're studying New Orleans. We also practice our calendar skills by clapping and stomping through the days of the week. We read a poem daily and we do a 'syllable stomp' to count the number of syllables in each word. Sometimes, I have a student stand on a desk so that others can see his feet stomping to the count of the syllables. My kids love to learn this way and, most important, they do learn. They retain and accomplish much more than they did before I started this practice."

Sophie's wisdom of practice resonates with brain research, helping both the girls and boys in her class. Let's go deeper into that research and look at why the physical movement (and the music used to stimulate and guide it) works for kids' brains.

Improving Synaptic Connections

When kids move around, neural pathways develop and brain cells connect. When you see babies and young children—beginning at birth—stretching, rolling, running, spinning, swinging, climbing, pushing, and pulling, you are seeing human nature utilizing movement to build neural highways in the brain. Sophie's movement activities fulfill the call of the natural brain—especially a boy's brain—to increase cross-hemisphere connections to translate learning into language.

Developing the Corpus Callosum

As we learned in Chapter One, the corpus callosum is a relay station that sends electrical signals between the two hemispheres of the brain. The female brain has more neural connections in this relay station, but movement, especially cross-lateral movement, creates more healthy connections in this relay station for both boys and girls—and this is crucial to learning. As this brain center develops, integration of activity and insight from both hemispheres of the brain increase. This brings the whole brain to focus more actively on a particular learning task. Music, too, is a whole-brain activity, and when coupled with movement, it can be a positive factor in bringing the assets of both hemispheres to a task.

Improving Attention Spans

Physical movement stimulates curiosity and curiosity increases attention. Certain neurotransmitters, such as dopamine, are associated with a pleasurable feeling and are stimulated by physical activity and novelty. All of these effects on the brain help a learning mind stay out of "zone out" rest states—improving note-taking, memorizing, listening, and learning. The increased dopamine can mean decreased impulsivity, thereby improving classroom behavior, especially for boys and some girls. Class becomes "fun" in a way that reduces trouble and improves learning.

Improving Learning Through More Circulation and Respiration

Movement increases the brain's ability to pay attention, solve problems, and retain information—not just because of stimulation to neurotransmitters, such as dopamine, but also because of increased blood flow and oxygen to the brain. Whereas the female brain naturally has a higher rate of blood flow in the brain, movement can help many boys to get their blood moving at an increased rate, helping with attention and focus. As movement increases heart rates, oxygen levels increase, making the brain more alert.

Decreasing Negative Stress

Some stress in life and learning is a good thing. The stress increase when taking an important test can actually help a child do better on the test. At the same time, certain stressors decrease learning ability. This "negative stress"—for instance, the stress that comes from being constantly reprimanded—is reduced by physical movement. Sometimes teachers will ask us, "But how can that be? If kids are moving around, won't teachers be constantly yelling at them because of classroom chaos? Won't aggressiveness and impulsivity just increase?"

In fact, ten years of action research conducted in over a thousand schools shows just the opposite. As long as the teacher lays out ground rules for movement, and enforces consequences when kids abuse the privilege, movement actually reduces aggression, decreases boredom (and the ensuing acting out), motivates learning, and decreases both students' avoidance of learning and their fears that they can't learn.

And sometimes, movement activities result in spontaneous laughter—a stress reducer in itself.

Wisdom of Practice: Teachers Talking

The use of physical movement to enhance learning is age-old, of course, but also newly discovered in each generation of teachers. When teachers talk about utilizing movement, some will say, "Hey, when I was a student, we just sat and memorized." Then another teacher will reply, "Yes, but we had a lot of recess, and we also spent a lot more time outdoors as kids than kids do now. We moved around more during any given day." Some teachers will feel a little bit intimidated about using movement. "I can't do it," they might say. "It will disrupt learning."

Physical movement is a best practice that not every teacher can or may want to jump into right away. You as a teacher may want to get mentoring and training in how to introduce movement to your classroom; you may want to team up with others who have successfully done so.

Here are three wonderful voices of support for all of us. These teachers are using physical movement, and their students are reaping the rewards.

Second-grade teacher Kari Reams reports, "I got a brilliant idea from a teacher at the beginning of the year to help build community. She had the students write their names on a piece of paper and wad it up like a snowball. Then, they got on opposite sides of the room and threw the snow balls. Then, they picked up a snow ball, not their own, and returned it to the rightful owner. I decided to try this game and my kids LOVE LOVE LOVE it. I've adapted it for so much of their learning. For instance, my students write math facts on a piece of paper, wad it up, throw it in the middle, and then pick up other kids' snowballs. The one they pick up is the problem they have to solve. They love the game so they are more motivated to solve the problem. Another application is to write word work patterns on pieces of paper and do the game with those; also, vocabulary can be snowballed. Whatever snowball the kids get, they have to answer, define, or read the word or problem on the paper."

As Kari has noticed, movement is often associated with games. Music can be playing in the background during the game, or the game just goes on in its own boisterous way. Teachers like Kari discover that the game provides order and discipline to the movement activity. The kids want to play the game well, so they may move around in quick movements and have some fun while making, throwing, and retrieving snowballs, but then they settle down to accomplish their task with movement-inspired energy and acumen.

Third-grade teacher Kendall Manning became conscious of the need for physical movement when she noticed some of her students seeming to fall asleep in class (they were zoning out and getting bored). "I noticed it in both boys and girls but it is much more prominent in boys. The boys tend to get off task by staring into space, doodling on their papers, or playing with their pencils. Girls are able to attend more and longer than boys based on my observations in my classroom." She is a good teacher and knew that she wasn't necessarily "at fault"—she wasn't a particularly boring teacher! She realized there was something going on in the way her kids' brains were and were not attending to her lessons. She followed the lead of other teachers who utilized physical break times in lesson plans.

In her words: "For those moments when everyone seems to be falling asleep in the classroom, I have all the students stand behind their chair and get moving. There are times when I have the class walk laps around the room (minus the closet—it's too tight in there). Other times, I tell the kids that I want them to do multiple things like five jumping jacks, five push-ups, and five sit-ups. There are times when I let them just move around . . . it doesn't matter what they are doing as long as they are moving! It is always a special treat to throw some music into the mix also! They get back to learning well after the movement time. As with many strategies on student learning, both the boys and the girls respond positively from brain breaks and getting up and moving."

What Parts of the Brain Are Involved with Movement?

Basal ganglia: a collection of structures inside the cerebral cortex that is important to voluntary movement, including well-learned movements (such as walking), and sensation.

Cerebellum: regulates balance, posture, movement, and muscle coordination.

Frontal lobe: responsible for reasoning, emotions, judgment, and voluntary movement.

Motoneurons: neurons responsible for movement. The cell bodies of these neurons are located within the brain or spinal cord and the axons are located in muscle fibers.

Kendall's plan is simple and takes up little time, but gets the kids learning again.

Lori Nuelle, an experienced K–5 teacher, practices her own form of this technique. She reports: "When students have the wiggles and are unable to listen to learn, we stop to do our 'exercises.' I use this with grades K–5 and they love it partly because they know what is coming and also because I make it into a listening game. I have everybody stand up, and we stretch to the sky. Then I start the chant, "Pump your arms up and down. Pump your arms to the ground. Put your hands on your waist, turn, turn. Forward, side, other side, back." I repeat this last set several times and mix it up like side, other side back, back or forward, back, side, forward. When I observe most of the students listening and waiting for the next direction, I repeat the whole chant with them and then we sit down and proceed with the directed lesson."

Physical movement is your ally, and easy to utilize in your daily lessons. To feel comfortable, you may want to move around a little more yourself during the day. If your students are paying attention to you as you talk to them, and you are moving around the room, they have to be moving too! You, too, might enjoy the dopamine rush of feeling your own body and brain fully present in the moment. Your kids will enjoy seeing you practicing your own "dance" of learning, your own jumping jacks, snowball tossing, stretching, and clapping.

Common Teacher Questions and Concerns

"Is there enough room in my classroom for movement?"

If you work in an open-space school, you may feel limited by your proximity to other classes and the need to stay fairly quiet. In this case, explore other options, such as the gymnasium, cafeteria, or break-out space. Whether you are short on space or select an activity requiring more space, you can also consider taking the learning to the playground. In fact, the playground (weather permitting) allows for even greater movement with less concern about noise levels. Outdoor light enhances learning. Children in Minneapolis, Minnesota, receive, on average, only thirty minutes of natural outdoor light a day. Students in San Diego don't fare much better with sixty minutes a day of outdoor light, yet greater exposure to natural light decreases stress and depression, and improves academic performance. As we learned in Chapter One, exposure to natural light may have a positive impact on estrogen levels in girls, helping them maintain a more even emotional keel.

Children also need plenty of time outdoors to allow the visual cortex to develop properly. Outside is where children can develop the visual skills needed to judge and accurately estimate depth and distances. Mary Rivkin, author of *The Great Outdoors: Restoring Children's Right to Play Outside*, tells us there is one very basic reason that children need to experience being outside as much as learning will allow: humans evolved in the outdoors.

"When am I going to find time in the day for movement activities?"

We know there is never enough time in the day! Let's start by first considering the purpose of the movement activity. Is the purpose of the movement simply to change the physical state—to increase oxygen, blood flow, and heart rate, thereby reenergizing or relaxing the body and brain for learning? If this is the case, the activity can be kept rather brief and simple, thus eliminating a lot of setup, transitions, or materials. These activities can be done on the spot and can be sprinkled in as you see that your students need them. And remember, once the learning brain is recharged, whatever comes next is more likely to stick.

On the other hand, is movement being used to teach, practice, review, or assess the content that you are delivering? In this case, movement is not a break from learning; in fact, there is no need to separate movement activities from content activities. You do not have to choose between movement *or* science *or* reading—because movement is done while the child is reading or doing a scientific activity. Let your students move right around their chairs, if they need to, while you are teaching comprehension, grammar, math facts, states, and capitals—you name it. We'll give you a number of ideas for how to do this in a moment.

"Won't I lose control of the class?"

This is a common concern of all teachers—voiced even more often by teachers with a lot of boys in their classes. Anyone who starts throwing out the balls and beanbags in class without preparation is bound to have a classroom management problem. Make sure to take a look at how comfortable you are with increased movement and noise in your classroom. There is definitely a difference between unproductive, off-task noise and the noise that is generated by students fully engaged in an exciting task. If students are not doing what they need to be doing, it will be obvious to you, and you will have the opportunity to guide and direct their learning. Conversely, during more sedentary classroom activities, students could be off task or daydreaming, and you may be less likely to notice; just because they are quiet doesn't mean they are learning.

Before introducing movement activities to your classroom, allow plenty of time to discuss and rehearse the procedural expectations. Just as you practice how to line up and walk down the halls, practice how to move safely in the classroom, how to toss those balls or beanbags, and how to stop the activity quickly and focus on the teacher. And if a child misbehaves while moving around, there must be consequences. Make sure to promulgate new and fair rules for movement, and enforce them.

"The principal won't think we're learning unless the students are sitting quietly at their desks."

Principals never took a class in how boys and girls learn differently either! This might be the perfect time to bring out this book and offer to share what you've learned. The bottom line is that, in your classroom, there should always be high-quality student learning. Content is the "what" of teaching. The "how" of teaching is the strategies that you employ to get students to learn that content. When you are incorporating movement strategies into learning, it is important that you don't lose track of the content.

In all teaching and learning scenarios—and especially those that incorporate more creative methods, such as movement—be sure to ask yourself some important questions. If you can knowledgeably discuss the "what" and "how" of instruction in your classroom, you will ensure that your instruction stays on track and you will be better prepared to help other teachers, administrators, and parents understand the effectiveness of what you are doing:

- Are the students clear about what they should know and be able to do as a result of this lesson?

- Do students understand how the movement activity helps them to acquire, rehearse, or review the concept or skill?

- Are the noise and movement directly related to the teaching and learning activities (are students on task or off task)?

- What evidence do I have that students are mastering the concepts or skills?

- What evidence do I have that students are motivated and engaged in the learning process?

Finally, consider doing some action research of your own. Teach lessons with and without movement and then track the level of students' retention. Also, consider taking success data from schools across the country (see www.gurianinstitute.com/success.html) to show your principal or other administrators. Brain-based strategies, such as movement, really do work, and that has been proven all over the world.

Practical Ideas for Your Classroom

"Learning is experience," Albert Einstein said. "Everything else is just information." These are wise words for all of us.

Quick "Anytime" Brain Breaks

The following activities can be used whenever you want to bring the energy level up—or just prior to introducing an important concept. The activities are simple and short, yet succeed in waking up the brain and priming it for learning.

What's Your Name?   Have students stand up and spell their first name in the air with their right elbow, their middle name with their left elbow, their last name with their head. Try other names or words with different parts of the body. Observation note: Do the girls and boys use their bodies differently as they do this activity?

Cross-Laterals   These activities get both sides of the brain talking to one another. Have students pat their right ear, shoulder, or elbow with their right hand, and vice-versa. Cross-laterals also include marching in place white patting opposite knees or heels.

Pass It Along   Have students stand in a circle, cross their arms and hold hands. As in the previous Cross-Laterals activity, having the students cross their arms helps them stimulate cross-hemisphere brain connections, "waking up" both sides and getting the brain more ready to learn. Start the group off by squeezing the person's hand to the right. Each person then passes the squeeze along to the next person. Try it again by sending a squeeze to the left and the right at about the same time. See if both squeezes can come back to the first person. A variation is to pass along a funny face or a funny noise.

Hand Fidgets   Provide a variety of "fidgets," small items with interesting textures like bean bags, Koosh balls, gel-filled toys, smooth stones, rubber tubing, and strips of Velcro or furry fabric. Allow students to get a fidget if they need one. This is especially helpful to boys, who find it more difficult to keep still while doing seat work. Girls, due to their heightened sensory intake, will enjoy the textures of the various fidgets.

Standing Up   If you are round-robin reading or reviewing for a test, consider doing it standing up. Caution: Don't make students stand "at attention" as this can cause similar problems as having to "sit still." Allow modest movement while students stand so long as they are not distracting their classmates.

Do the Wave   Charge the group up by having them do "the wave." Stand up, stretch the arms high and shout, "Whooo!" in a wave-like pattern across the classroom. Send the wave back. Use this activity as a way for your students to give a group response to a question, saying "Yesssssss" or "Nooooooo."

Freeze Frame   Turn on lively music. Have students stand and dance in place, silently, to the music. When you stop the music, have them freeze and look at everyone else's positions. Resume music and continue. Variation: Let students take turns leading this activity, with their classmates following their movement. Observation note: Are there observable differences in how the girls lead and how the boys lead? If so, how are they different?

Fruit Picker   Have your students stand up with arms stretched out and reach to pick imaginary fruit from a tall branch, alternating from left to right, crossing midline. They can also pick lower down and then close to the floor. Variation: Let students identify their favorite fruit, tell where it grows (in a tree, on a vine, for example) and lead the group while they pick.

Positive Vibes   Have each student turn to a neighbor, shake hands or high-five and say, "It's great to be here!" or "It's great to be alive!" or "It's great to be smart!" Have them continue until they've made contact with at least five others. Observation note: Do the students more often seek out members of their own gender, or are they pretty "coed" in their choice as they move around the group? Does this choice pattern look different depending on the grade level?

Mirror Image   Have each student face a partner. One partner moves slowly and carefully, while the other partner mirrors his or her movements. Make it more difficult by having one partner do several movements while the other partner just watches. Then the second partner can try to repeat the movements. Try pairing the students up boy-boy, girl-girl and boy-girl. Is there a difference in how the activity goes depending on the gender pairing?

Crazy Faces   Agree as a group on three crazy faces, and have students pair up, and stand back-to-back. Each partner makes one of the three faces, and then both turn around to see if their faces match. Have the pairs repeat the game. How many times do they match out of ten tries? As in the Mirror Image activity, change the pairings to be same gender and coed—ask the students if it was easier or harder one way or the other. Ask them why.

Adaptable for Any Subject Area

These are good for both boys and girls in different ways! Activities that encourage the boys to engage their verbal processing resources are definitely a plus to developing literacy skills. Having girls engage their spatial resources gets them to "exercise" less-used resources that will become more and more important as they move into more abstract content and higher math.

Scavenger Hunts Have students move about the room to find different colors, numbers, textures, items with different vowel sounds, and so on. Variation: After the students have gone around the room finding the designated items, have them return to their seats and see how many they can "list." Let them list by either making a list of words, or by drawing pictures or representations of the items—their choice. Note how many choose to list words and how many use drawings. Is there a gender difference in this activity? What would be the benefit from requiring words one time and graphics the next?

Musical Chairs Play musical chairs with a twist. Instead of eliminating the student left standing, he or she answers a question about the content you are teaching. The game continues so that many students get to answer a question.

Ball Toss Review For review, have students sit in a circle and pass a ball or a beanbag. Ask a review question and toss the item. The child who catches it answers the question and throws it to someone else. That student must then pass it to someone who hasn't yet had a turn. This continues with the teacher asking review questions and the students passing so that everyone gets a chance.

Finger Spelling Kids love sign language. Teach them the alphabet in sign and have them practice their spelling words or content vocabulary with finger spelling. Sometimes teachers wonder if knowing sign language leads to "cheating" on spelling tests! From the feedback we get from teachers, this isn't a problem, and the benefits far outweigh the risks!

Action Storyboard   Have one student act out an aspect of something learned today. Have that student freeze and have another student act out another concept or skill. Continue until several students have contributed to the storyboard. Can the rest of the class go back and retell the story from the beginning?

Show Me What You Know!   Have students divide into small groups. Identify several key words, skills, or concepts from the lesson. Have teams develop a song and dance routine that incorporates the concepts. Have them perform for the class.

Language Arts

Stimulating the neural connections between the spatial right brain and the verbal left brain is a key to improving literacy performance for boys. All children benefit from increased activity, and the following are some ways to make language arts learning fun. When we're having fun our chemical plant responds in healthy ways!

How Can You Move?   Give half of your students a red index card with a verb on it. Give the other half of the students a blue index card with an adverb on it. Have students find a partner so that every pair of students has a verb and an adverb. Cue music and ask students to move in the manner specified by their cards—skip slowly, walk quickly, dance gracefully, and so on. Have some pairs demonstrate for the group. Observation note: Do you see any difference in how the girls and boys respond to the movements they have been asked to do? Do you hear any boys saying they aren't going to "dance gracefully?" In this kind of activity, you might see signs of socialization or stereotyping that children bring with them from their world away from school.

Alphabet Games   Give each child a laminated card showing a letter of the alphabet. Have students close their eyes and mix themselves up, and then put themselves in order as quickly as possible without talking. Have the consonants touch a vowel as fast as they can. Call out words and have the students organize themselves to spell the words. What words can they create?

Back on the Job   Tape a spelling word to each student's back—don't let the student know his or her word! When you say "Go" have students pair up and give each other definitions until the partners guess the words on their backs. Set a time limit. At the end of the time say, "Stop." How many got their words? Switch the words and play again—repeat as long as the students seem engaged. When you finish, have the students return to their seats and ask some questions about the process: Which partner made it easiest to guess your word? What made it easier? As you process this activity, see if any gender differences show up.

Physical Phonics   Post consonant or vowel sounds in your classroom or on the playground. Have students move in a way that you have instructed them (hopping, jumping, and so on) to the letter that matches the sound you give them. Make it more difficult by giving them a word and having them move to the correct vowel sound (such as long "a," short "e") or beginning or ending consonant.

Spelling for Fitness   Have students pair up with each other's spelling lists. One student gives a word and the other student does push-ups, pull-ups, or sit-ups while providing the spelling. Try having the students spell the word forward and backward. If students are doing a pull-up, they should try to hold it until they spell the word both ways. For push-ups, you might have them do one push-up for each letter of the word. Caution: Be sure to include physical activities that are less demanding so that students with any physical limitations can be successful. For instance, including toe-touches makes room for students who might be sitting in a wheelchair, or have an arm in a cast!

Attack of the Stickies   Divide students up into four or five different groups and give each group a different colored pad of sticky notes. Give them a letter sound and have them write the name of an item in the room that contains that sound (such as short "a" sound, long "o" sound, or a beginning or ending consonant sound). Once they've written the word on a sticky note, they should affix the sticky note to the item. Give them several sticky notes and then count them up to see which group found the most items with the sound. Try making three varieties of teams: all boys, all girls, coed. See if there is a difference in how the teams engage in the activity.

Vote with Your Feet   Designate opposite corners of the room as "strongly agree" and "strongly disagree." After reading a story passage, provide students with statements about which they can formulate an opinion. Have students move to one of the corners or somewhere in between, depending on their level of agreement. Have them defend their position to other students. Have students in the corners try to talk the students in the middle into coming to their corner. Observation note: as you proceed through the activity do the groups tend to take on any gender difference as they move from one answer to the next? Is it different depending on the grade level?

Mathematics

Taking math off the page is a plus for both boys and girls. Boys are able to use their strong suit, spatials, to learn. Girls, who tend to use their spatial skills less during elementary school because they are so successful using their strong suit, verbal skills, benefit from the opportunity to exercise their spatial skills.

Jumpin' and Hoppin'   Practice identifying odd and even numbers by providing students with a number and then have them hop in place if it is an odd number, or jump in place if it is an even number.

Multiples in Motion   Practice multiples of the numbers one through nine by clapping and snapping! Give students a number and ask them to count from one to twenty. Here's the trick: Students are to count by clapping and saying the numbers in their head. When they reach a multiple, they should snap and say the number out loud. For example, multiples of three would be *clap, clap, snap*-"three"; *clap, clap, snap*-"six"; and so on.

Buzz-Fizz   A harder variation of the multiples game makes this a group game. Have students stand in a circle and number off. Then, starting at student "one", have the students count, replacing the multiple of three with "Buzz": "one, two, buzz!; four, five, buzz!" When they have this down for several numbers add complexity by having them work with multiples of two numbers (such as three and four) by saying "buzz" for one of the numbers and "fizz" for the other number: "one, two, buzz!"; "four, fizz! buzz!"; "seven, eight, buzz! nine, fizz!"

Human Number Line   Give each student a card with a number on it, either a positive or negative integer (for example, -15 through $+15$, if you have thirty-one students). Hand them out randomly and see how quickly students can put themselves in order. A variation is to put a sticker on each child's back so that children don't know their own numbers. Have them work silently to properly order themselves. When you start adding and subtracting positive and negative numbers, have one student move up and down the human number line to solve the equation. Observation note: You might find it's harder for most of the girls to do this activity "silently" than for most of the boys. Girls will tend to want to talk, using those verbal resources!

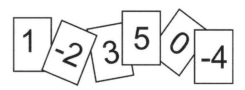

More Number Lines   Have students stand along a number line from 0 to 25 (or up to the number of students in your class). Have all the even numbers jump forward, all the odd numbers jump back; have all the numbers divisible by three snap their fingers, all the numbers divisible by four wave their arms in the air, and so on.

Are You Right?   Have students use their arms to create an angle. Have other students decide if the angles are acute, obtuse, or right. More advanced students can estimate the degrees of the angle. Observation note: Do the boys seem more confident in their estimates than the girls do? Added spatial abilities tend to make it easier for boys to make guesses like this—and make girls less confident in their guesses. An activity like this is good exercise for both, especially with no negative response to inaccurate guessing.

Human Clock   Have students use their arms to represent a time and have their partners try to figure it out. This is a great activity for boys because of the movement while learning; it's a great activity for the girls because it moves their learning into the spatial realm, which we want them to exercise more.

Sign Language Math Facts   Teach students the signs for the numbers 1 through 20. Agree on an operation: addition, subtraction, multiplication, or division. Have student pairs stand back-to-back. The first partner forms two numbers on his or her hands and says "Go." The students turn to face each other and the second student tries to give the answer to the math fact as quickly as possible. Trade roles and repeat several times and then change the operation.

Frequency Table   Have students "graph" themselves. Have students line up along an x-axis based on their month of birth, favorite ice cream, favorite TV show, number of teeth lost, and so on. For an extra challenge, have them organize themselves without talking.

Science

Science lends itself to learning while moving as well as, or better than, any other subject—to the benefit of both boys and girls. Making science fun also helps engage those girls who feel less comfortable with science than language arts. Here are a few science-related activities to add to your toolbox.

Solids, Liquids, and Gases   Designate a large area for students to move around freely. Then confine them to a smaller space to move around and then to a very small space to move around. Discuss their ability to move (as molecules) in a large space (like a gas) versus a small space (like a solid).

Orbiting Planets   On the playground or in the gym, set up cones to mark the sun and each of the planets. Have students line up along the orbit of one of the planets. When you say "Go," have them bounce a ball as they orbit the sun, remembering to maintain a constant distance from the sun. To add complexity, have them turn their bodies as they go to represent the day-night cycle. Why did it take some students longer to get back to their starting place? Observation note: This is a great activity for girls, whose gross motor development is usually less advanced than their fine motor skills when they start school. Moving and bouncing a ball at the same time are great for gross motor coordination and will build confidence. Be sure the balls are large enough so that the students won't have any trouble maintaining control as they orbit.

Push and Pull   Have pairs of students hold each other's hands and try pushing and pulling under different conditions, such as with one student sitting down while the other stands, or with one student leaning back against a wall, or with one student in socks and the other in shoes. What are the variables that affect each application of force?

It's Electric!   Have students create parallel and series circuits on the floor with a rope and laminated cards representing resistors, circuit breakers, bulbs, and so on. Have students walk around the circuit and discuss what is happening at each point of the circuit.

Viruses & Antibodies   Using an outdoor space or space in the gym, have students play "walking tag" in a large area. Designate several students as the virus (taggers). Give them sheets of red construction paper. The rest of the students are healthy cells. When healthy-cell students have been tagged, they then become the virus and begin to tag other healthy-cell students. Introduce antibodies. These are students who cannot be tagged by the virus. Give them sheets of yellow construction paper. Their job is to tag the virus-cell students so that those students return to normal cells. What happens to the proportion of students who are healthy cells and viruses when antibodies are introduced?

Social Studies

Many teachers we work with have voiced concern that social studies is getting less attention in today's classrooms because it isn't as relevant to standardized test. In tomorrow's (and today's!) world, however, the content of social studies becomes more and more important, as we prepare our students to compete and succeed in an ever-flattening world economy. Making social studies active and fun is a way to stress that it's important, while using the content to reinforce literacy skills.

Vote with Your Feet   This activity is set up the same way as "Vote with Your Feet" in the Language Arts section (see page 27). After reading or discussing a social studies topic that involves a moral or ethical dilemma, provide students with statements about which they can formulate an opinion, and have them "vote" by going to the designated areas of the room. Observation note: You might try selecting some issues based on gender—such as, "It's important to have both men and women become nurses." See if there is any gender pattern in the response. This is a great opportunity to discuss how roles for men and women have evolved over time.

Clue Sort   If you are studying continents, draw the outline of each continent on a piece of paper and put the papers on the floor in different places in the room. Hand out index cards with clues and information about the different continents. Have students work in groups to sort all of their cards out and place them on the correct continent. This activity can also be used with states, presidents, and other social studies concepts. Variation: To appeal to both verbal and spatial learners all along the brain-gender spectrum, make some of the clue cards with words and some with visual clues.

Time Travelers   Establish a timeline in a large area. Give students different dates and have them move in different ways to the place on the timeline that the event took place.

Community Builders   Have students use ropes on the floor to delineate a small community. Have them decide where to place the schools, homes, and businesses within the community and label the locations with signs. Have them analyze traffic flow by moving about on the streets of the community. How might they plan their community to ensure smooth traffic flow? Variation: Divide into groups by gender and have each group brainstorm what businesses they would like their community to have and come to consensus on their top five (or ten?) choices. Taking turns, ask each group for a business they selected, then let the other group decide if they would add it to their list or not—if they add it, they must remove one of their own choices. Is it possible to come to consensus between the groups on the final list for their community? What are the biggest differences? Does one group show more willingness to compromise?

Find the Facts Game   Prepare ten questions from content material you are or will be studying. Put one question each on a sheet of paper and tape them to the wall, window, bookcase—anywhere in the room (and extend into the hallway if possible!). Don't put them in order! Using a printed sheet of information or pages from a text that contain all the answers to the questions, have the students divide into teams of three players: one researcher (who will look through the information for answers to the questions); one recorder (who will record the answers in a numbered list); and one runner (who will go get the number and question from the posted questions—not writing them down!—and come back and tell his/her team the question). Tell the students to be as quiet as possible so other teams can't hear them finding the correct answers. First team to collect all ten questions and find the answers raises their hand. You can stop at this point, or let all teams complete the game before stopping. Make the information sheet and questions age appropriate for your grade level. The example below has worked well with upper elementary.

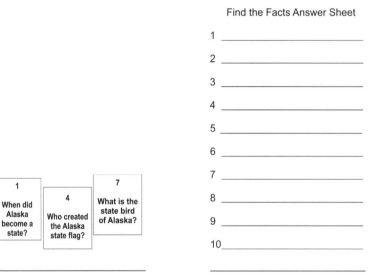

**Fig 2.1: Sample
Question Sheet**

**Fig 2.2: Sample
Answer Sheet for the
"Recorder"**

Interesting Facts About Alaska

Alaska has been called America's last frontier. Russian whalers and fur traders on Kodiak Island established the first settlement in Alaska in 1784. Alaska's name is based on the Eskimo word "Alakshak," meaning great lands or peninsula.

In 1867 United States Secretary of State William H. Seward offered Russia $7,200,000, or two cents per acre, for Alaska. On October 18, 1867 Alaska officially became the property of the United States. Many Americans called the purchase "Seward's Folly." Alaska officially became the 49th state on January 3, 1959. In 1926 13-year-old Bennie Benson from Cognac, Alaska designed the state flag.

Alaska is a geographical marvel. It is the United State's largest state and is over twice the size of Texas. Measuring from north to south the state is approximately 1,400 miles long and measuring from east to west it is 2,700 miles wide. When a scale map of Alaska is laid over a map of the 48 lower states, Alaska extends from coast to coast. The state of Rhode Island could fit into Alaska 425 times. Nearly one-third of Alaska lies within the Arctic Circle. The state boasts the lowest population density in the nation. The state's coastline extends over 6,600 miles. Juneau is the only capital city in the United States accessible only by boat or plane.

The discovery of gold in the Yukon began a gold rush in 1898. Later gold was discovered at Nome and Fairbanks. Alaska's most important revenue sources today are oil and natural gas. Alaska accounts for 25 percent of the oil produced in the United States. Prudhoe Bay, on the northern Alaskan coast, is North America's largest oil field. The Trans-Alaska Pipeline moves up to 88,000 barrels of oil per hour on its 800-mile journey to Valdez.

The fishing and seafood industry is the state's largest private industry employer. Most of America's salmon, crab, halibut, and herring come from Alaska.

The wild forget-me-not is the official state flower.

The willow ptarmigan is the official state bird.

The Sitka spruce is the official state tree.

Dog mushing is the official state sport.

Gold is the official state mineral.

The four-spot skimmer dragonfly is the official state insect.

At 20,320 feet above sea level, Mt. McKinley, located in Alaska's interior, is the highest point in North America. Seventeen of the 20 highest peaks in the United States are located in Alaska. The Tongass National Forest is the largest national forest in the United States.

In 1915 the record high temperature in Alaska was 100 degrees Fahrenheit at Fort Yukon; the record low temperature was –80 degrees Fahrenheit at Prospect Creek Camp in 1971.

WRAPPING UP THE MAIN IDEAS

- Providing movement opportunities in the classroom is critical for proper brain development and preparing the brain for learning.

- Movement increases blood flow and oxygen to the brain. In addition, a number of neurotransmitters are released that enhance learning.

- Movement increases focus, motivation, and memory.

- Students often learn best by doing.

- Movement can be used to energize, relax, focus attention, and facilitate transitions.

- Music that is upbeat will increase the heart rate, give students an adrenaline boost, and encourage more energized movement. Music that is slow and soft will help kids slow down.

- Movement opportunities can be integrated across the content areas so that students are learning while they're moving.

- Take classroom management issues into consideration up front. Good planning and proper preparation with students will ensure that movement activities are successful and enjoyable for all.

Make It Visual

3

Tools to Support Your Spatial Learners

. . . words and pictures can work together to communicate more powerfully than words alone.

—William Albert Allard

HAVE you noticed how many words we all use in a day? Researchers studying gender differences in language use report that women tend to use about three times as many words as men in a day. This is understandable based on what we learned in Chapter One about the difference in verbal resources available in the male and female brain. This research has important implications for the elementary classroom.

We are creatures of language, and our classrooms rely on words to make sense. At the same time, have you noticed how many of our students don't quite get our verbal directions, or learn something quickly when images are attached, but zone out (their eyes glazing over) when we teach certain things just with words?

A classroom that is friendly to both boys and girls will use words and other spatial-visual aids for the communication of skills, concepts and understanding. While the primary method of delivering new knowledge might still be linguistic, we are practicing the best teaching for all possible combinations of talents when we integrate nonlinguistic modes of delivering knowledge. Brain-based research shows us that many students—especially many of our visual-spatial boys—are better able to think about and recall knowledge when it is presented in both ways. Research emerging from a number of schools trained in how boys and girls learn differently reveals that (1) student brain activity increases with the use of visual-spatial tools, and (2) very importantly, the effects on student academic achievement are positive.

? DID YOU KNOW? Visual-Spatial Learning Works!

In *Classroom Instruction That Works,* Marzano, Pickering, and Pollock identify the use of "Nonlinguistic Representations" as one of the nine instructional strategies with the highest probability of enhancing student achievement across all subjects and grade levels.

Following up on the research of Marzano et al., our Gurian Institute wisdom-of-practice research shows that when "the lens of gender" is applied to linguistic and nonlinguistic tools, all learners enjoy the addition of variety of tools to the school day, and there is a subgroup-specific gain among those many boys and some girls whose strengths lie in the visual-spatial domain.

If you could do PET or SPECT scans on the students in your class, you would find that a number of them have greater cortical activity devoted to visual-spatial thinking than others do. These students, many of whom are boys, are adept at watching objects move through space, rotating objects in space in their mind's eye without a physical model, solving visual puzzles, and engaging in higher-level reasoning in the spatial domain. The highly-verbal classroom setting, comfortable for many girls, does not fully or consistently engage these spatial abilities in the learning process. This can present a real mismatch between the delivery style of the teacher and the learning style of the child, a mismatch that can alter a learner from a "good student" to a "bad student." Visual-spatial aids can alleviate a large part of this mismatch.

Understanding the Strengths of Their Brains

We're all probably familiar with the idea that we learn better when we approach new learning from a position of strength. This is commonly called a "strengths-based approach," which emphasizes that the process of acquiring new learning should originate from the identified strengths of the learner's individual mind. Those strengths become the foundation for building new skills, especially in areas that pose a specific challenge. Students who work from a position of strength have better self-esteem, become more confident in their abilities, and are more willing to take risks—all essential ingredients for successful learning. This is obvious, a teacher might say, what's your point?

Our work in the area of male-female brain differences has shown us that many of us have tacitly decided to use linguistic teaching to such a degree that we forget to apply strengths-based learning. We forget how different students' brains can be. Many of us are so verbal ourselves as teachers that we assume, even if unconsciously, that every kid learns the way we teach. We have bought into a hidden message of contemporary teaching, which says "using your words" is the best way to learn.

The work we do with helping boys has taught us that especially when kids are in the first few grades, "use your words" is somewhat overused in our schools. The male ancestors of these youngsters used very few words—they learned by being in the outdoor world, the world of physically moving objects, the world of visual and spatial stimulants. Many of our youngsters—both boys and girls—need more of what their brains are biologically primed for in order to be strong learners.

When you employ the kind of visual-spatial learning tools we'll provide in this chapter, specific subjects can be better acquired by your students. Here's an example of how it happens—from the brain's point of view.

Brain imaging research from Australia has recently established that when a student's visual-spatial activity in the right, spatial side of the brain is increased during learning, subjects are better able to tackle left-sided language problems. Researchers began their research by looking at where mathematical learning takes place. They found that mathematical estimations and approximations are done in the right hemisphere, whereas mathematical computations are done in the left hemisphere. By stimulating the spatial side of the brain, both kinds of math could be learned better. These findings led Dr. Gary Egan, of the Howard Florey Institute in Melbourne, to call on all teachers and schools to make sure we are teaching to both the more verbally oriented left side of the brain *and* to the more spatially oriented right side. And remember, in Chapter One we learned that boys tend toward a right-hemisphere preference.

Reading, Writing, and Your More Spatially Oriented Students

Have you ever wondered why some students use more sensory detail in their writing than others? There can be many reasons for this, of course, one of which is quite simply that some brains store and process sensory details better than others—especially when those details are linked to words. Other brains need more spatial stimulation to remember and then write about the details.

Often your male-brained students and your bridge-brain female students will experience and store less sensory detail than your more female-brained students and more bridge-brain males. In general, the female brain excels in more acute, detailed perception of sight, sound, and touch. Additionally, females have more neural connectors between "feeling" centers of the brain and "thinking" centers of the brain, rendering them more able to put their emotions and feelings of sensation—touch, smell, taste, sight—into words.

If you read the stories that teachers proudly display in the hallways outside their rooms, you will see some real variation in the number of words and the amount of sensory detail in the stories posted—often there is a gender difference. Girls, with their increased sensory intake, will tend to use about 25 percent more words than boys, who tend to be more concise and use less written description. Do a little research yourself. Look at the great work hanging in your school's halls and count the words. Does this gender difference show up in the work you observe? Of course there are exceptions to all generalities, but in our work with schools this pattern tends to hold true.

Does this mean boys can't become better at this kind of writing? This is a reasonable question, and the answer is, of course, no. Boys can be wonderfully descriptive writers, but they generally need more support in generating sensory detail and rich descriptive language. Stimulating them in visual-spatial ways helps them to access more sensory and emotive words and experiences.

Think about that child who stares blankly at a piece of paper and struggles to get his thoughts onto the paper. This student's strengths may well reside in the visual-spatial domain versus the verbal-emotive domain. Whatever writing this child does produce may be short and cryptic. Maybe it lacks complex sentence structure or descriptive language. Perhaps this child crumples up his paper and dissolves into tears. The more we evaluate children's performance from a "production" expectation, the more boys will feel frustrated with language arts.

Perhaps most painful, in an ultimate sense, for this child and his school is that he will constantly be assessed as a bad writer. This could negatively affect him and turn him off to school, possibly throughout his life.

Now ask this child to draw pictures of what he wants to write about. Give him some time to do that. Have him draw a storyboard or quick chart of his subject matter (many practical ways of doing this are provided later in this chapter). Perhaps in your fourth-grade classroom the assignment is to write about what happened over the weekend. On his storyboard the student can draw panels with colored pencils about the drive his family took, what they saw, whom they met, what amazing (or boring) things happened.

Now have him write his paper. Watch how many more sensory details he now uses—he refers back to visual-spatial cues (his drawings) and has a wonderful cache of sensory details to put in a paper.

A number of our target schools have used this technique and seen positive improvement in student grades. It is a nonlinguistic tool that engages their more active visual-spatial centers in the right hemisphere, and thus supports the work asked of their verbal centers in the left.

While girls may be less attracted to this tool because of their higher level of comfort in working with words, encouraging girls to participate in this activity gives them needed practice in exercising their spatial resources. This is great preparation for later in school when those resources will be required.

Some Questions to Think About

- How might a different approach help the child who can't get his or her ideas on paper?

- How can we support students in organizing their thoughts without having to generate words to get started?

- How do we honor this child's visual-spatial abilities and make those abilities work *for* the child instead of against him?

- What strategies might a teacher employ to assess students in a way that is not so entirely dependent on the child's acumen with language?

The answer to these questions is in striking a better balance between the verbal and the visual in your classroom. The answer lies in finding more ways to *make it visual!* As you answer the questions and put into practice some of the strategies in this chapter, you'll find these sorts of gains for both boys and girls:

Students who organize ideas visually first, verbally second will often gain in outline and organization of papers (resulting in better grades), which in turn increases student confidence and ultimately motivation to learn. Many of these students will be boys.

Students may well show a quantitative increase in sensory detail and descriptive word choice. These strategies may stimulate mental images of the five senses, allowing for better recall of experiences when unimpeded by slower language formulation, helping level the field for boys whose language development is often a year to a year-and-a-half behind that of girls.

Student vocabulary and retention of new concepts may improve. Some of our schools have noticed that concept reinforcement through visual-spatial modalities can improve achievement. Students demonstrate understanding through pictures or symbols in ways that clearly require comprehension.

Parent involvement in student learning also increases—which is a big gain for the student's achievement. Kids go home and say, "I can draw before I write," and parents will often admire the drawing and be "drawn into" the helpful process of motivating the child to do better. One parent recently said, "It's like I see a light at the end of the tunnel now. There's a tool for writing that helps my son enjoy writing. Writing isn't something my son hates, and something that makes us as parents think he will fail."

> **What parts of the brain are involved in visual-spatial thinking?**
>
> *Hippocampus:* stores and processes spatial information. It acts as a *cognitive map*—a neural representation of the layout of the environment.
>
> *Right hemisphere:* governs spatial thinking. Memory is stored in auditory, visual, and spatial modalities.
>
> *Corpus callosum:* the neural highway that exchanges information between the right and left hemispheres of the brain.
>
> *Supramarginal gyrus:* involved in spatial meaning and it is the part of the brain that guides action—for example, in coordinating how a person moves his or her hand toward a glass of water.
>
> *Thalamus:* the brain's key sensory relay system.
>
> *Occipital lobes:* the two areas (one for each hemisphere) that process visual information.

Practical Ideas for Your Classroom

Albert Einstein said this about his learning experiences: "Some thoughts do not come in any verbal formulation. I rarely think in words at all." We are not all Albert Einstein! But in your classroom there are a lot of girls and boys who need us to help them think in visual and spatial ways before they move to words. Who knows what great theories these kids will generate, if the strengths of their minds, and variety of learning methods, find fruition in their classrooms?

Following are a number of nonlinguistic tools you can use throughout all phases of the instructional process—from initial introduction of a concept to assessment of students' understanding. While a number of these could incorporate the use of words, we want to emphasize the use of nonverbal ways of conveying thoughts and ideas initially. It is also crucial to emphasize the importance of these ways of communicating not only to reading and writing learning, but also to math and science learning. Some of these strategies can be immediately applied to helping more verbally oriented students (often many girls) stay with the process of spatial reasoning, so that they can get the mental practice they need to succeed in areas of math and science that are nonverbal.

As you read and use this practical ideas section, you'll notice a division into four main strategies that you can add to your toolbox. The following will cumulatively provide more visual-spatial techniques in your classroom:

- Graphic organizers
- Physical models
- Symbols and pictures
- Mental imagery

Of course, a key to making your class less verbal-dominant is to talk less—and that starts with you! This can be especially challenging for female and bridge-brain male teachers, who tend to be more verbal. For that reason, we've also included some sample lesson formats that decrease the amount of teacher-directed instruction time and increase the amount of student activity time.

Graphic Organizers

A visual representation of knowledge, a graphic organizer structures information and arranges it in a way that visually represents the organization of ideas. It can be used to compare, contrast, sequence, or expand ideas. Once formulated, the organizer provides a record of a student's thinking, a "roadmap" for how to proceed with an assignment or project, and a review sheet for what has been learned. Following a lesson, the process of trying to capture the main concepts and transpose them into a graphic representation is a high-level synthesis task in itself.

There are two distinct kinds of organizers: those that use words (linguistic) and those that don't (nonlinguistic). Depending on the needs and preferences of your students, you may wish to offer one or both kinds to your class. For some students, and especially for boys and bridge-brain girls, just having the spatial representation of their thoughts, even if it requires them to use words, is very helpful. For other students who get bogged down with spelling or letter formation, you may wish to stick to graphic organizers that allow them to avoid using words—at least initially—to ensure the smooth flow of ideas from the head to the paper. Selecting the right tool for the job is absolutely critical, and we've provided examples here of different kinds in practice. These examples fall into four main ways that graphic organizers organize and represent knowledge. Remember—while all of the graphic organizers can be used effectively in all subject areas, not all organizers achieve the desired results for a specific task.

Hierarchical Organizers   This organizer includes a main concept and sub-concepts under it. For example, a fourth-grade class may be studying the main events leading up to the American Revolution. Another example of this organizer's use might be in writing a persuasive essay, such as about why people should not smoke. The three sub-concepts would be the three main reasons for not smoking, along with details to support the reasons.

Name _____ Date _____

Flow Chart

Write your topic at the top. List steps or events in time order.

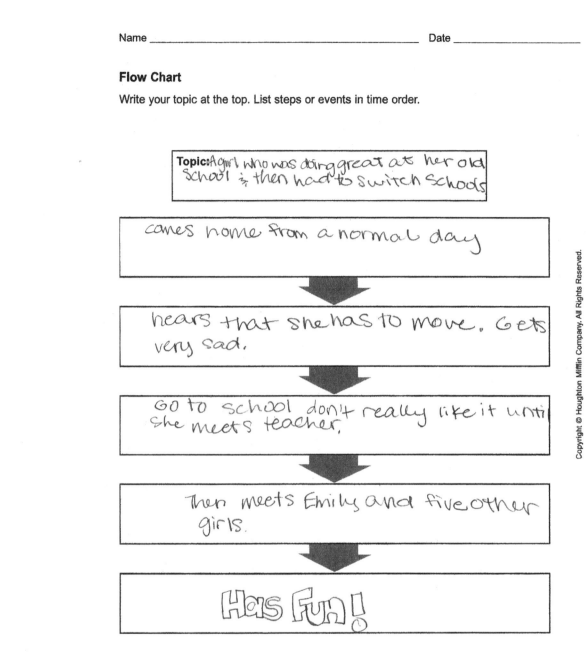

Topic: A girl who was doing great at her old school & then had to switch schools

canes home from a normal day

hears that she has to move. Gets very sad.

Go to school don't really like it until she meets teacher.

Then meets Emily and five other girls.

Has Fun!

Conceptual Organizers This organizer includes a central idea or category about which you want students to develop supporting facts, such as examples or characteristics. This is an excellent organizer for descriptive writing. For example, students might be describing a place that is special to them. They can use the concept map to record the details gathered by their five senses—what they see, hear, feel, smell, and taste. Venn diagrams aid in tasks that require comparing and contrasting. Because conceptual organizers do not impose a sequence of thoughts, they are good for brainstorming but not necessarily for creating the linear structure required for a report.

Name _____ Date _____

Idea Wheel

Label each section. Then write or draw ideas in each section.

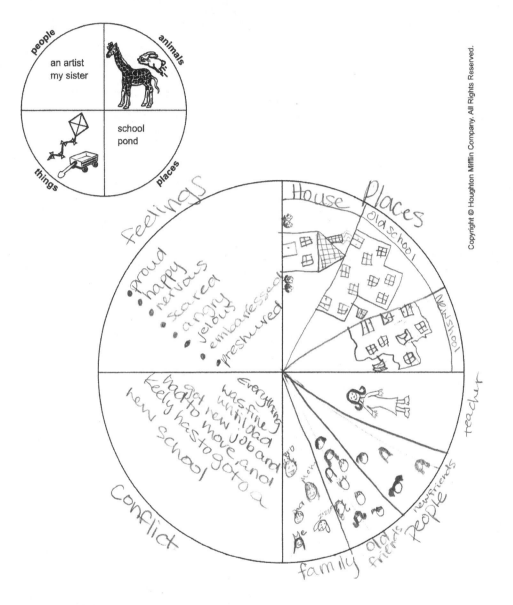

Sequential Organizers   This organizer arranges events in a chronological order. It can be used for beginning-middle-end, cause-effect, chronology, or problem-solution. Another kind of sequential organizer is a storyboard, which works especially well for younger children. It is similar to creating a comic. The sequential organizer can be used effectively for recounting historical events or telling a fictional or nonfictional story. The rising action plot line can be especially helpful for students writing fiction, creating a sequential timeline of events that helps students visualize how the problem in the story is established, climaxes, and then resolves.

The Brighton Red Playoff Game

Every player was about as happy as you could get.

We went home and celebrated our big win.

We made the tackle. We had to beaten + ho be the best team in the league.

We got a saftey and were everything by 3 but we had to stop them.

Off we went the opening kickof we all knew we had a tough game ahead.

Cyclical Organizers   This organizer can be used to illustrate a single main event or a series of events representing a process that has no obvious beginning or ending. Examples of such a process would be a life cycle, the water cycle, photosynthesis, or even the steps in long division. The cyclical organizer is an excellent tool for initiating discussion of prediction and sequencing skills, showing how one step or event leads to another. Cyclical graphic organizers can easily be used with pre-readers by using pictures instead of words.

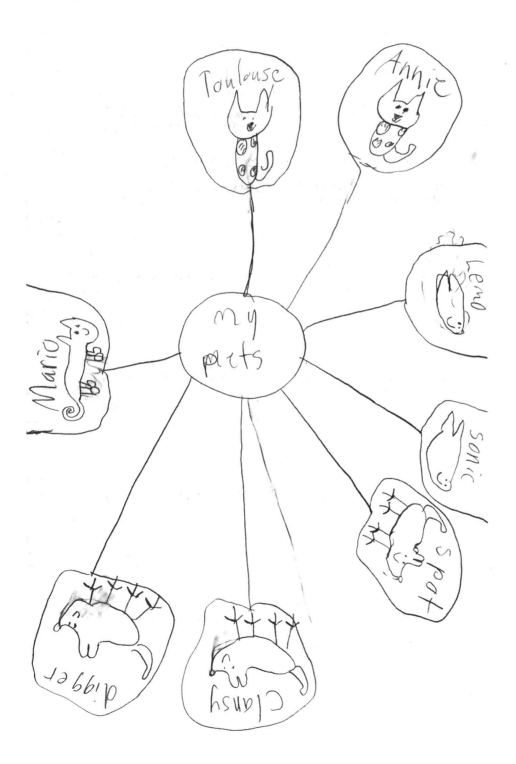

Finding the Right Organizer for the Job   Teachers at Douglass Elementary School did a lot of thinking about the different reasons for writing. They knew that developing a common instructional language was essential in creating the building blocks for success as students moved from kindergarten through fifth grade. Once they had decided on the different purposes of writing (see box below; also see Chapter Seven for greater detail), they started asking themselves precisely how students were being taught to plan their writing. What graphic organizers were other teachers using around the building? Should they be teaching and using the same ones? Were some graphic organizers better than others for specific kinds of writing?

What resulted was a clear awareness that they needed to give students "the right tool for the job." If kids need a hammer but are given pliers, it is hard to accomplish the desired task and the tool ends up being used in a manner for which it wasn't designed. The same is true for graphic organizers.

The whole point of a graphic organizer is to help a student organize his or her ideas and information in a spatial manner. The spatial representation of ideas then can serve as a scaffold to take the students to the next level—when they will put their ideas and information into a logical verbal sequence. We really defeat the purpose when graphic organizers don't provide students with a spatial representation that will flow well into the verbal structure that we want them to produce.

Let's take an example: You want students to write about the sequence of events leading up to the Industrial Revolution. You want them to first capture their ideas with a graphic organizer. In this case, the graphic organizer should help students *organize sequentially.* Therefore, using a conceptual organizer, such as a "mind map" or "spider web," will not be effective in organizing the child's ideas in any sequence. The student will be able to generate a number of ideas, but the ideas will not be presented in the sequential manner that the final report requires.

On the other hand, if you are trying to get students to brainstorm sensory detail for a descriptive piece, you may wish to use a conceptual organizer—which, unlike a hierarchical organizer, gives each idea surrounding the main theme equal weight. It does not impose a certain order, and provides for an unlimited amount of "branching," as the student extends and deepens his or her thinking. In this case, the conceptual "mind map" may be the perfect choice.

Students can become incredibly sophisticated in understanding the purpose of their writing and in selecting the best graphic organizer. As they are ready, include them in this important decision-making task so that they have many tools at their disposal and are able to choose for themselves "the right tool for the job."

We have provided below Douglass Elementary's recommendations for which types of organizers are most effective for each of the "eight purposes of writing."

Douglass teachers decided to keep the purposes simple and straightforward. This was done intentionally so that students could easily learn the names of the different purposes of writing starting in the early grades—as well as to help teachers to be consistent with their instructional language.

EIGHT PURPOSES OF WRITING

Developed by Douglass Elementary School, Boulder Colorado

- *To Narrate (fiction):* usually organized chronologically. Use a sequential organizer, such as a timeline. A "circle" story (coming back to where it started) lends itself to a cyclical organizer.

- *To Narrate (non-fiction):* usually organized chronologically. Use a sequential organizer, such as a timeline.

- *To Describe:* focuses on descriptive sensory words. Use a conceptual organizer, such as a mind map or other non-sequential or non-hierarchical organizer.

- *To Report:* usually organized in a typical five-paragraph essay format. Use a hierarchical organizer that will break down the main topic into sub-categories followed by details. Depending on the content, a cyclical organizer (especially in science) may also work well.

- *To Explain (what and why):* this type of writing lends itself to a hierarchical organizer with a main idea, supporting ideas and details.

- *To Explain (how-to):* this is a sequential, first-second-last sort of piece. Use a sequential organizer such as a storyboard so that students can draw out the steps.

- *To Persuade:* a hierarchical organizer works best; however, the sub-topics are not always of equal importance or weight. If you want students to make their best point first, use a hierarchical organizer that shows the relative "weight" of each of their arguments.

- *To Express:* poetry comes in many structures and forms. Depending on the type of poetry, the organizer will vary. Typically, conceptual organizers work best to draw out the descriptive language and sensory detail.

Making Physical Models

Physical models are concrete representations of the concept that is being learned. Physical models are often used in math in the form of manipulatives, including Unifix cubes, counters, and fraction tiles. During math instruction in particular, the use of manipulatives can be very beneficial to female students who tend to do less of their thinking in the spatial domain. Giving girls practice in the spatial domain with the aid of manipulatives can enhance their visual-reasoning skills, as well as their mathematical thinking.

In addition to math manipulatives, physical models can be used more broadly to demonstrate abstract concepts in concrete ways. An excellent example of the use of physical models to teach integers is demonstrated by Kathy Campbell, a third-grade teacher:

> Kathy is preparing to teach the concept of positive and negative numbers to her third graders. She has considered a variety of physical models, including money, a frog jumping along a number line, a building with many floors, and others. In the end, she decides to use a model of a tall building. She begins her work with the students by labeling the floors of the building they have built together out of blocks. The model of the building is set up on a table so that students can see below the base of the building. Students readily accept the underground floors as "below zero." Kathy and her students then explore what happens as little paper people enter an elevator at one floor and ride to another floor. This is used to introduce the conventions of writing addition and subtraction problems involving integers $3 - 5 = -2$ and $-2 + 7 = 5$. Students are presented with increasingly difficult problems. For example, "How many ways are there for a person to get to the second floor?" If the paper people start on the ground floor, the response might be to "Go up 2 floors" or something more complicated like, "Go up six floors, down five floors and up one floor." Working with the building model allows students to generate a number of observations. For example, one student noticed that "any number below zero plus that same number above zero equals zero."

Another example, this one of making physical models in social studies, has been provided by Pam Unrau's third-grade class:

> Pam's students are learning the major landforms of Colorado. After discussing typical Colorado landforms, such as plateaus, valleys, mountains, and plains, each student creates an outline of the state on a piece of tagboard. Pam has the students help mix up a large batch of salt dough and they portion it out to all of the students. With Pam's direction and guidance, students use the salt dough to create the different elevations in

the state. Later, when the salt dough has dried, students label the cities, peaks, national forests, and other points of interest on their maps.

———————

Mary Jo Barbeau's second graders learn about the town of Boulder, Colorado in the 1800s through the construction of physical models:

Students are working fervently in Mrs. Barbeau's class today. They are using pre-cut pieces of wood to build their 1800s-style log cabins. Roofs, windows, and doorways are positioned just so and held in place with Elmer's glue. Parent volunteers scurry around helping with the construction phase of the project. Students have already taken digital pictures of themselves in 1800s-era clothing, printed out the pictures in small scale, and affixed them to popsicle-stick stands. These paper dolls will be used to populate the homes and village. This activity is a culminating project. Students are applying what they've learned about life in 1800s Boulder to the construction of their replica town. Each student has already composed a written piece, which is hanging on the wall above the place where their town will be displayed.

When all of the cabins are finished, the students decide where to place their cabins in their village, which has been created atop two large tables and is complete with fields and a stream. Interestingly, the girls select sites close to the center of town where they can be close to their

Second graders Maddie and Liam build physical models for their 1800s Boulder town.

Second grader Alex works with his classmates to build their model town. Note that the students' written pieces about old-town Boulder are matted and "published" on the wall behind their model town display.

friends. The boys select sites on the edge of town where they can be closer to the open fields so they can "run around and hunt and stuff," or by the river so they can fish.

The following is a list of ideas for using physical models. Some of these ideas work well for use in the classroom. Others make great homework projects:

Language Arts

➡ Use a variety of noodles and beans to represent the punctuation marks in a sentence. Punctuate sentences on the floor or on the overhead projector. Glue them onto construction paper to punctuate a sentence that the students have written. See how *macaroni is used below:*

❝ See how high I can fly ❞ said the bird.

➡ Students themselves can become a physical model. Have students dress up as their favorite character in a book and act out a scene.

➡ Before writing, have students create clay models of the main characters of their story.

➡ Have students form their spelling words with clay. Other students can trace the models with their finger for tactile input.

Mathematics

➡ Use manipulatives whenever possible! This can include tangrams, pattern blocks, counters, dice, fraction tiles, ones, tens, or hundreds blocks.

➡ Food is always motivating to students. Have students work with chocolate bars, cookies, graham crackers, and other food items to represent math concepts, such as fractions.

➡ Have students develop a better concept of large numbers like 100, 1,000, and 10,000 by collecting beans and displaying them in various sizes of jars.

➡ Have students use clay to illustrate important mathematical language concepts, such as "more than" and "less than," or to demonstrate their understanding of multiplication, division, fractions, geometry terms, and so on.

➡ Provide students with building blocks and have them build models to demonstrate their understanding of number patterns, such as triangle numbers and square numbers.

➡ Have students create a game board with cards and game pieces to demonstrate the concept of probability. Playing games builds neural linkages between the frontal cortex, the thinking part of the brain, and the limbic system, the feeling part. So, when kids are playing games, especially games that they have helped design, they are thinking and feeling—a good connection for them in their development.

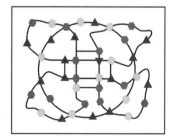

Science

➡ Have students create a model of an animal or plant cell using any materials they would like. Encourage students to be creative and then allow them to share their finished products with the class.

➡ To develop an understanding of how sound travels, have students build contraptions that will carry sound waves. Have them fill bottles with water to create a physical model for the different pitches of sound.

➡ To teach the phases of the moon through a concrete representation, give students a Styrofoam ball. Hold a light in the middle of the room. Have the students hold their Styrofoam balls towards the light and guide them to move them so that they create different phases of the moon (such as solar eclipse, full moon, half moon).

➡ When studying animals, have students use rope and a measuring tool to create a life-size outline of the animals on the ground.

➡ When teaching balance and motion concepts, give students a variety of materials and challenge them to build a model that balances an object on a fulcrum.

Social Studies

➡ After learning about communities, have students build their idea of a table-top utopian town. Depending on the age of the students, the technical requirements of the model can be more sophisticated.

➡ Have students construct a miniature battle scene from the Civil War or a company village during the Industrial Revolution.

➡ Have students pack a suitcase with memorabilia that would have been important to them at the time that their family would have emigrated to the United States.

➡ Have students each make a recipe from a designated time period at home. Have them bring the food in for a "feast," but first have a conversation about why those people chose these foods and methods of preparation.

➡ Create an artifact from the part of the world that you are studying, such as a didgeridoo from Australia or tribal shields from Africa.

➡ Create an outline map of the United States on the playground (the art teacher can be a resource here) large enough for the students to stand on or in a state. This can be used a variety of ways to play games and help students learn: names and location of state, path of major rivers, trails of westward movement, Pony Express trail, and many more. Kids have a great time painting the states too!

Using Symbols and Pictures

Having students create symbols and pictures to represent their knowledge is a powerful way to reinforce their understanding. It can be initially difficult to convey meaning without the use of words, so the exercise in itself can become a high-level synthesis activity. The students often appreciate the novelty and fun of developing pictures, symbols, and—even better—"secret codes."

You may want to start reading a book that includes symbols of some sort, such as pictographs or hieroglyphs. One good title is *The Lost Boy and the Monster* by Craig Kee Strete. This book includes the traditional pictures and text, but also includes symbols on every page that correspond with the story line. This provides a good model for how meaning can be expressed without words, and is a great exercise for both boys and girls.

Next, go ahead and try out this strategy. Start with a small-scale application of the strategy before launching into a whole-class project. For example, after a short verbal explanation of a new concept (such as the life cycle of a plant or the food chain), have students draw a picture or pictures to visually demonstrate what they just heard. Have them share their drawing with a partner, then continue with the lesson and repeat after several minutes.

Pictures and symbols can also be used prior to teaching a lesson as a way of assessing background knowledge. Post butcher paper on the wall and have students come up and sketch what they already know. When they're done, sit down and discuss the pictures and their meanings as a group. What do students already know about the topic? What new information do they want to know? Those ideas can be sketched as well. Remember: this is not art class, so make sure your boys and girls both know you want to know their thoughts, not a sample of their artistic talents!

A good example of a whole-class culminating project using symbols and pictures takes place in Bill Smith's and Anne Gibson's third-grade classrooms:

Today, the children are spread out across the floor in the classrooms and the hallways. Their colored pencils and markers are at the ready as they concentrate on their works of art. Long scrolls of blank paper have been taped together and are stretched across the floor. These are what the students call their "Learning Scrolls." Students are organized into learning groups, charged with conveying their knowledge pictorially about the language, culture, customs, dress, and homes of the Native American tribes that they have been studying. Student groups organize themselves differently but all must agree on how to go about sharing their knowledge with others without the use of words. Soon, they will share their completed Learning Scrolls with other students and display them in the hallway for others to admire.

Word Walls, and Integrating Pictures and Words

A Word Wall is a systematically organized collection of words displayed in large letters on a wall or other large display place in the classroom. It is a tool to use, not just display. Word walls are designed to promote group learning and be shared by a classroom of children as a resource. Pairing pictures and symbols with words is a great way to increase retention of new vocabulary in all content areas . . . and spice up your Word Wall!

If you don't already have a Word Wall, find wall space and start one. Word Walls make great visual resources in a classroom that can help kids get "unstuck" if they don't know how to spell a word or are looking for a good word to use. If you've already got a Word Wall going, expand it to incorporate content area vocabulary from math, science, and social studies. Too often, Word Walls only incorporate high-frequency sight words or words that children need help spelling. Since students write across the curriculum, make sure your Word Wall takes them where they need to go.

The next step requires enlisting your students' help. Have them create a symbol that depicts each word on your Word Wall. High-frequency words—such as "the" and "and"—do not need to be included. Look for other words on your Word Wall that convey meaning. Have students use a large index card to draw a symbol for each of these words and display the symbol next to the written words. This can be done each time you add a

swamp

Defenition: A swamp is an area of trees, mucky water and water animals. They are usually found on a Penniseula or near river deltas or near the ocean. Mainly Places w/ →

A fourth grader created this Word Wall definition and illustrations during their study of biomes.

word to the wall. If you already have dozens of words on your wall, have students work on adding symbols to the wall when they get time in class. Most important, have students explain how and why they created the symbol the way that they did.

Drawing pictures is a great way to "prime the pump" for boys and girls as they begin the writing process. The more detail and use of color, the better for getting those creative juices flowing. Instead of having students illustrate their work once they are finished writing, have students spend some time simply drawing as a way to get their thoughts down on paper. Linda Taht, a fourth-grade teacher, calls this process "planting seeds" and actively encourages students to sketch in their Writer's Notebooks.

Next time you look at student drawings, notice the detail that conveys thoughts about the characters, the setting, and the action. The drawings can also capture sensory detail that can be transferred into the children's writing. Conference with students about their drawings just as you would conference with them about their writing. Having students explain their drawings (and the story they depict) is an important step in bridging the nonverbal and the verbal. You probably won't have time to conference with each student at this phase of the writing process, so select a few of your reluctant writers to check in with. Have other students confer with each other. To facilitate their peer conferences, give

Zach, a fifth grader, created this watercolor picture before writing a descriptive piece about his favorite place.

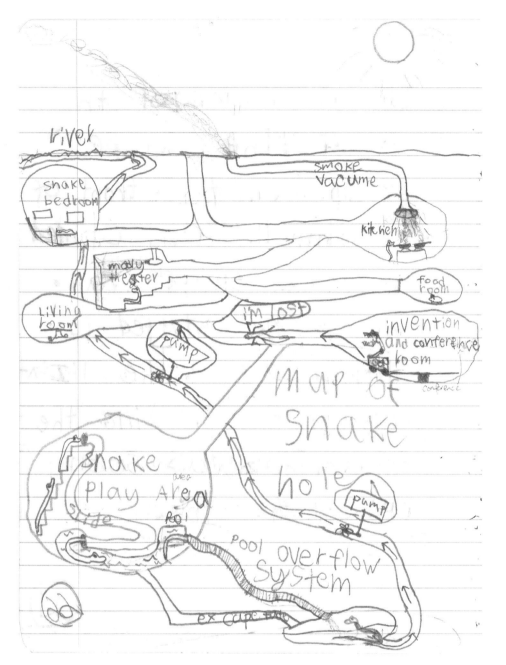

This is an example of a student's drawing that was done in the pre-writing stage to help the student organize his thoughts, increase imagery, and begin the process of transferring ideas to paper.

them some sentence stems to talk about such as, "The main characters are . . ." or "My story takes place in . . ." or "The most exciting moments of my story are . . ."

On p. 58 is a good example of how a teacher set students up for success in writing a "How-To" piece. Note that the layout of the page directs students to organize their ideas in a sequential, step-by-step manner. Additionally, there are places on the page for both drawings and writing. Students who are more visual can complete the sequence of drawings *first* and then go back and do the writing, using the drawings as an organizational "stepping stool" to the written language output.

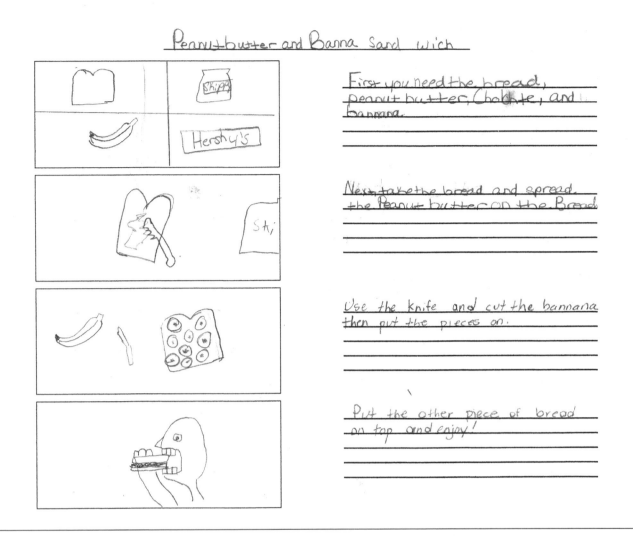

Second grader Hunter and fourth grader Austin collaborated on this writing piece about how to make a peanut butter and banana sandwich. On each page, the students drew the steps first and then wrote about them.

Drawing pictures can also be helpful for students as they write up lab reports in science. Encouraging them to make sketches in their lab notebooks will support them in developing well-written results and conclusions. With so much writing required in math class nowadays, it is helpful for students to first communicate their thinking in pictures and symbols before moving to their written explanations.

Remember that—especially in this day and age—visuals don't need to be created with crayons and markers alone! Employ technology, such as Kid Pix or Storybook Weaver, to assist students in creating digital graphics. Most kids will be even more motivated to write when they get to use the computer and a great drawing application.

Try These Activities in Your Classroom

Here are a few more quick-and-easy ideas to increase the use of visual teaching and learning strategies in your classroom. After teaching your students a lesson in a given content area, have them try one or more of these activities:

- Create a four-panel coat of arms to depict what they've just learned.
- Sketch a book cover that captures the main idea or problem.
- Draw a bird's-eye view map of the setting of the event or story.
- Create symbols for the key vocabulary they've learned.
- Create a comic strip retelling the events.

Mental Imagery

Mental imagery is the process of using one's "mind's eye" to create a mental picture of the knowledge being learned. Not only is this technique effective in reviewing information, it is also very helpful in enhancing sensory detail—something we know is especially important for boys. Give students' imaginations free rein! More cortical areas of their brains will be activated as they visualize a historical event, "see" themselves flying above a significant location, or replay a scene from a story in their heads. Once they can visualize something in detail, they can draw it out, talk about it, and then write about it more effectively. Not only will the engagement of the multiple brain pathways increase their memory of the information, it will increase the likelihood of effective retrieval.

Take, for example, this lesson in Mr. James's fifth grade classroom:

Mr. James's class has begun a unit of study on the rainforest. After learning about the ecosystem and animal life in the rainforest, Mr. James has the students close their eyes and imagine that they are walking through a tropical rainforest in South America. He has them "feel" the hot muggy air and the sweat running down the backs of their necks. He has them "hear" the buzzing of insects, the screech of the howler monkey and the call of the endangered quetzal. They "see" an iguana scurry across the forest floor under the cool dark leaves of the understory.

"Suddenly," Mr. James tells them, "You hear a strange sound in the distance. You hear the sounds of voices and loud machinery and the cracking of branches. You smell smoke. Would you be confused? Frightened? Curious? As you go closer, what might you see? What would you do?"

Yesterday I started buying supplies to make Valentine's Day cards with my kids. My girls are thrilled about doing this, but my son was not. After reading just 150 pages into The Minds of Boys, *I now understand that Ethan's brain is not programmed to enjoy this craft process like the girls. Instead we are going to make them on the computer. He is thrilled with this idea. If I had not read this book I would have insisted that he make Valentines with the girls because it is "fun"—and he would have been miserable. I am very grateful that I am understanding him better.*

—A mom

A first grader's story. Note the use of technology to craft a picture for his story. His work was then posted on the school's Web site to create a larger audience for his work.

<u>Mayan Temples</u>

They have deadly snakes that can kill people. But they can't kill special people. They pray to god because god is a special person.
By Ben

To increase students' ability to visualize text, Alicia Morris, a first grade teacher, had her students close their eyes and "paint pictures" in their minds as she read Dr. Seuss's *Horton Hears a Who*. After listening and visualizing, she had each student draw a series of pictures to depict what they "saw." On p. 61 is one student's finished product:

The power of visualization and mental imagery has been recognized for years by sports psychologists and athletes. K. Porter in *Visual Athletics* states,

The reason visual imagery works lies in the fact that when you imagine yourself performing to perfection and doing precisely what you want,

you are in turn physiologically creating neural patterns in your brain, just as if you had physically performed the action. These patterns are similar to small tracks engraved in the brain cells which can ultimately enable an athlete to perform physical feats by simply mentally practicing the move. Hence, mental imagery is intended to train our minds and create the neural patterns in our brain to teach our muscles to do exactly what we want them to do.

Ten-year-old gymnast Roxanne gives the following account of how she uses mental imagery prior to doing a complicated tumbling move: "I just visualize myself doing it perfectly. I have to picture myself doing each of the steps as if somebody videotaped it or something. I don't know how it helps me, but I do my twisting layout really well every time I visualize it first." Another strategy Roxanne uses: she draws a sequence of pictures depicting each phase of the tumbling move. The process of drawing out the steps and then referring back to them prior to tumbling has helped her to increase her confidence to the point that she began executing the tumbling move on her own. Roxanne is getting important practice using her spatial brain in both the visualization and the drawing activities!

In *Research-Based Strategies to Ignite Student Learning*, Judy Willis, MD states, "Neuroimaging of brains when students begin to *think* about a specific type of learning show activation in the area of the brain that controls that particular type of learning. For example, the front executive function areas become more metabolically active as subjects think of organizational strategies needed to prepare materials for a debate, even before they are given the debate topic." Clearly, the implications for visualizing what is to be learned or what has already been learned are powerful. Additionally, the technique is fairly simple to implement in that it does not require the purchase of new materials and requires only limited classroom time.

Following is an example of student work that is the result of a classroom exercise that included the use of mental imagery. Students were assigned to write a descriptive piece about a special place. For inspiration, students were given the choice of selecting a photo or creating their own mental images. Students were guided through the planning stages of writing to incorporate extensive sensory detail about what they could hear, feel, see, smell, and taste in their special place. Additionally, students used pastels to bring their visions of their special place to life.

Note this student's excellent use of similes, the five senses, and descriptive word choice to paint a clear picture in the reader's mind.

When I'm up on my zipline, I feel wonderful, excited. I see the gray wire that connects from the tall post to the wood frame. I see the bright, red handlebars, blooming black-eyed susans, and tall waving grass. My eyes also catch the colorful bushes and shrubs, and the dark, textured dirt. I hear a magpie's hoarse crow, the rustle of leaves that remind me of a cool, fall day when trudging through a pumpkin patch, picking out the perfect pumpkin. And beside me, I hear a beautiful butterfly, its yellow wings softly fluttering back and forth. I smell the fresh, open air, and the aroma of sweet honeysuckle. I feel the soft breeze that flows through the open field, making it seem as if it is a salty ocean, with

waves crashing against its shore. And as always, I feel the cold metal of
the handlebars as I zip, zip, zip down my zipline!!!

—Written by Allison, fifth grade

Talk Less! Sample Lesson Formats

We know that this is easier said than done. That's why we have provided
some sample formats for you to consider as you are planning your instruction. Hopefully, these can serve as a framework to help you break up the
verbal components of a lesson into smaller, "bite-sized" chunks that can
be better assimilated by your students. Also, the framework can serve as a

reminder of how frequently we need to get students engaged in tasks *other than listening.*

"Talk-Less" Basic Lesson Format

Step 1: Get Their Attention	1–5 minutes
Step 2: Why Is This Important?	2 minutes
Step 3: Direct Instruction: Content	10 minutes
Step 4: Activity	5–30 minutes
Step 5: Debrief and Closure	5–15 minutes

An Overview of the Steps

Get Their Attention: Use the first few minutes to grab students' attention and get them fully "in the room." Use this time for an energizing brain-break to help them disengage from what was happening at recess or in the hallway and to check in with their current surroundings.

Why Is This Important? Helping students see the connection between the content and the "real-world" is discussed in detail in Chapter Seven. Tell them they'll be solving a puzzle. Ask them if they have concerns about the environment . . . or civil rights . . . or whatever it is that you are going to be teaching. A visual demonstration in a science class can be a great way to pique students' interest.

Direct Instruction: This is your opportunity to present content in a teacher-directed manner. Not all lessons require this, but some do. Limit your instruction to 10–15 minutes and be sure to include lots of visuals.

Activity: This is the time that you need to change the physical and mental state—time to stop talking at them. Get them involved in social interaction, such as a movement activity or drawing, that will reinforce the concepts that are being taught. Be sure to offer visual-spatial dominant activities so that you are strengthening both linguistic and nonlinguistic thinking at this time.

Debrief and Closure: Bring students back together so that the key content of the lesson can be highlighted and clarified. Allow students to share their observations. Find connections with previous learning, various subject areas, with real-life experiences and with humor. Students could also be given quiet time to sketch what they've heard and then share.

Depending on the age of your students, this lesson frame will need to be modified. For example, in a kindergarten class, the structure may need to look more like this:

Modified Format for Younger Students:

Step 1: Get Their Attention	1 minute
Step 2: Why Is This Important?	1 minute
Step 3: Direct Instruction: Content	5–10 minutes
Step 4: Activity	10 minutes
Step 5: Debrief and Closure	5 minutes

If you find yourself needing to deliver a larger amount of content with older students, you may wish to further modify the lesson framework to be more like this:

Modified Format for Older Students / Lecture:

Step 1: Get Their Attention	1–5 minutes
Step 2: Why Is This Important?	2 minutes
Step 3: Direct Instruction: Content	10 minutes
Step 4: Brain Break or State Change*	1–3 minutes
Step 5: Direct Instruction: Content	15 minutes
Step 6: Brain Break or State Change*	1–3 minutes
Step 7: Direct Instruction: Content	15 minutes
Step 8: Debrief and Closure	5 minutes

---

*See Chapter Two for activity ideas (movement, social interaction, and music work particularly well).

WRAPPING UP THE MAIN POINTS

- Many students have strengths in the visual-spatial domain. This strength area is often under-utilized in the typically highly-verbal classroom setting.

- Students can use their visual-spatial strengths to scaffold them to success in verbal tasks, such as reading and writing.

- Research shows that a strong positive correlation exists between student achievement and the use of nonlinguistic tools, such as graphic organizers, pictures, symbols, physical models, and visualization.

- The key to decreasing the reliance on the verbal domain is to talk less. It's important to explore ways to restructure classroom lessons accordingly.

Empower the Learner

Giving Students Choice and Control

4

A good book for a boy is one he wants to read.

—Tom Moloney

MANY students don't subscribe to what we offer them to read in school. Too often, certain kinds of literature are discouraged in the classroom, the very kind a student might like. Sometimes, parents will say, "But my child likes to read at home—why is it a problem at school?" Girls in school are often reading material that does not touch them, inspire them, or resonate for them. Boys in school are often in the same boat.

Teachers all over the country are reporting changes in this generation of readers. They report many kids just not paying enough attention to their reading, falling behind in assignments, not doing their language arts homework, and generally not liking to read quality material. Teachers often feel quite disconcerted, even paralyzed. Compounding this feeling is the sense that every year kids are watching more TV, playing more videogames, spending more time on the Internet, or with iPods or cell phones—as one teacher put it, "Reading is passé to them." This situation creates anxiety in us as teachers—we know that while technology has changed much about how we function in today's world, it is still a "reading and writing world." Kids need to be competently literate if they are to make it in their future workplaces and lives.

There are a number of successful ways to solve the "crisis in literacy" that is discussed (with good reason) throughout the industrialized world in this new millennium. We will provide a number of practical and research-based strategies in this chapter. One of the important foundations for many of these strategies is the brain-friendly idea that if the students feel a natural and appropriate sense of control and choice making in their reading and writing, they are more apt to be more engaged and to accomplish the skill building that comes with both.

Neurologically speaking, "attention" is a process of selecting the most relevant information from an overwhelming mass of sensory input around us. How are we to compete with the distractions of the young person's world of today? The secret lies in understanding what it is that gets and keeps students' attention. We can come to this understanding—and exploit it in quality ways as teachers—without losing literature, and the love of words.

Why Giving Choice to Students Works

While the focus of attention of any human being obviously begins with survival—the body's physical need for food, shelter, and clothing—it moves quickly to two areas of experience that directly affect reading and writing:

Self-Made Choice. This is the ability to make a choice between two or more options on one's own and to follow through on the choice made.

Novelty. There is an area of the brain that responds to novelty, exerting a major influence on learning. This area, the substantia nigra/ventral tegmental area (SN/VTA), is structurally connected to the hippocampus, the brain's learning center, and the amygdala, the area where emotional information is processed. Activating this area through novelty—new and unexpected experiences—motivates the brain to engage, explore, and respond. These are all things we want the learning brain to do!

A number of schools and teachers have improved their students' literacy scores and basic enjoyment of reading and writing by factoring in the importance of self-made choice and novelty. These teachers have developed plans of action that fit with student's primal needs, plans that offer students choice and novelty when possible, thus engaging the attention centers of the brain, and better ensuring personal interest in a topic or resource.

This successful approach is based in connecting brain research with long-term studies on what builds reading success in students. Different research bases have come together recently to show that when learners feel that they are an important part of the process, their interest and accountability go up and retention increases dramatically.

To check these findings for yourself, you might acquire Jeff Wilhelm and Michael Smith's *Reading Don't Fix No Chevys.* Their two-year study showed that male students considered to be problem or reluctant readers in the classroom actually had very rich literate lives outside of school. These

---

What parts of the brain are responsible for attention and choice-making?

Reticular activating system: filters all incoming stimuli and makes the decision about what should be attended to or ignored.

Limbic system: a group of interconnected deep brain structures involved in a number of functions, including emotion, motivation, and behavior.

Left frontal lobe: exercises conscious control over one's thoughts to allow for focusing attention, prioritizing, and problem solving.

Amygdala: sensory inputs converging in the amygdala inform a person of potential dangers in the environment. The amygdala also helps us notice and attend to novelty.

students did not reject literacy. What they did reject was "school literacy." When these students were given choice and novelty, they "rediscovered" literacy.

Fourth grader Izaak is a perfect case in point. Izaak reports the following when asked how he would rate his enjoyment of writing, on a scale of 1 to 10:

> Well, at school I would rate writing a 1. At home, I would rate it an 8. It's because at home, I make up all these games. I need to write down the directions and stuff so that I remember how I made the games up and how to play them. At school, I mostly have to write about stuff that the teacher tells me or about stuff that I'm not really interested in.

Harrison's rasipe for
Barf
5 Bat eyes fras and new
2 cat tungs Hottly spisted
10 drigin clas made of irn
3 Human brans vary fluffy
4 galins of car oil very spicey
Light nig bolts very bright
600
999,999 wigley wams
1 stingy tow
15 dead mice

mix it well
and eat with liver.

Sometimes, giving students more choice and allowing for novelty means being able to stomach some unappetizing topics, such as third grade Harrison's "Rasipe for Barf."

Practical Ideas for Your Classroom

What is it that engages your students in reading outside of school? Ask them—and then get some of that reading material into your classroom! This really works. Don't be surprised if your students' responses include newspapers, magazines (such as *Sports for Kids, National Geographic,* or *Popular Mechanic*), instruction manuals, comics, and text or e-mail messages. You may not want some of this in the classroom, and you are the final authority, but the most important thing, especially for your most reluctant readers, is to get students reading, and reading often.

One elementary school we worked with that had significant gender gaps in literacy in the fourth and fifth grade proclaimed one day each week "Free Read" and allowed students to bring personal reading material for use during a time set aside for choice reading. The boys tended to bring articles from the sports section of the newspaper, comic books, and paperback books from the *Captain Underpants* series. The girls tended to bring a variety of book series (including *Captain Underpants!*) and young teen magazines. Students were allowed to sit at their desks, recline on the carpet, sit at work tables—in other words, choose where to read! After a few weeks, the teachers began offering a short period at the end of the choice reading time for students to share what they liked about their chosen free reading material—the end result was that the overall volume of reading went up all semester.

Giving Students Choice in Reading

Here are some basic tips to consider when increasing choice and appeal in your reading program:

- Assist students in choosing what to read.

- Encourage students to read a variety of genres.

- Don't use reading activities as a time filler.

- Allow students to read a wide range of materials in class.

- Have students recommend books to each other and to younger students.

- Get to know your students' outside interests so you can find books they'll like.

- Allow opportunities for students to physically act out what they read (for example, put on a short play), or make something connected to the content of the text.

The Harrison School District Gifted Services Division has developed a number of tools for teachers to use in the classroom to expand choice options for students. One good example is shared by Rachel Laufer: a Novel Choice Board.

After or during reading, students are asked to select one activity from each column to complete. If they don't find an activity that appeals to them, they can propose one to the teacher. You will note that the menu of activities offers a variety of activities, including visual-spatial tasks, verbal tasks, musical tasks, and so on.

Character Analysis	*Plot Analysis*	*Setting Analysis*	*Novel Response*
1. Choose two main characters in the novel you are reading. Using a Venn diagram, compare and contrast the personality traits of those two characters.	2. Describe the problem or conflict existing for the main character in the book. Tell how the conflict was or was not resolved.	3. Research and write a two-page report on the geographical setting of your story. Include an explanation as to why this setting was important to the effect of the story.	4. Find a song or a poem that relates to the theme of your book. Explain the similarities and differences using quotes from the book and the song on a poster.
5. Choose one character in your book to interview. Create ten questions that you would like to ask your character. Pretend that you are the character and answer the questions.	6. Compare and contrast the conflict of your book with another book that you have read before. Compare your similarities and differences on a poster of the two books.	7. After reading a book of history or historical fiction, make an illustrated timeline showing events of the story and draw a map showing the locations where the story took place.	8. Make models of three objects that were important in the book you read. On an index card attached to each model, tell why that object was important in the book.
9. Plan a party for at least four of the characters in your book. To do this, you must: (a) design an invitation for the party telling what kind of party this will be; (b) tell what each character would wear to the party; (c) tell what food you would serve and why; (d) tell what kind of games or entertainment you will provide at the party.	10. Stories are made up of conflicts and solutions. Choose three conflicts that take place in the story and give the solutions. Is there one that you wish had been handled differently?	11. Imagine that you have been given the task to conduct a tour for the town in which the book you read is set. Make a tape describing the homes of your characters and the places where important events in the book took place. You may want to use a musical background for your tape.	12. Create a board game based on events and characters in the book you read. By playing your game, members of the class should learn what happened in the book. Your game must include the following: a game board, a rule sheet and clear directions, events and characters from the story.
13. Write a diary with at least seven entries that one of the story's main characters might have written before, during, or after the book's events. Remember that the character's thoughts and feelings are very important to the diary.	14. Make a children's book retelling the plot of your book as it might appear in a third-grade reading book. Be sure that the vocabulary you use is appropriate for that age group.	15. Build a miniature setting of a scene from the book. Include a written explanation of the scene.	16. Write a scene that could have happened in the book you read, but didn't. After you have written the scene, explain how it would have changed the outcome of the book.

Offering a rich and varied mix of materials and being mindful of students' reading preferences can go a long way towards building an engaging and inviting reading environment for your students. In addition to the traditional materials, be sure to include: fiction, non-fiction, non-print resources such as CD-ROMs and bookmarked Web site pages, how-to manuals, a wide range of genres and formats, and easy-to-read books for building fluency.

Also, consider books with strong visuals. Currently, there are books on the market that combine photography with computer-generated images to create vivid, realistic pictures of fictional scenes. One such example is the Robert Gould *Time Soldiers* series. These books tend to be especially appealing to boys with their focus on adventure, risk taking and action.

Selecting Books with and for Your Students

When selecting books for your classroom or library, look for books that

- Reflect images of the students themselves—what they aspire to be and do
- Expose students to strong male or female role models with positive character assets
- Contain information that students will remember and use later on—funny lines, jokes, scores, and so on
- Come in a series—getting students "hooked" on a series is a great way to keep them reading
- Are action-oriented, especially if the book starts at a climactic point
- Are humorous, edgy, or unexpected

If you haven't already, ask your students to recommend good books! Let them affix stickers to the spines of the books they choose. You may want to have two different stickers—one for the books that girls recommend and one for the books that boys recommend.

Also, you can have your students create "trading cards" of their favorite books. Give them blank index cards, preprinted with general categories and space for comment. Plan a time for them to share and trade their cards, encouraging each other to discover new favorites.

Talk to your school webmaster about creating a "Book Review" page for students. Let students create reviews of books that they would like to share with their peers. This can include text and original art, encouraging students to read, write, and create!

Form a student committee to help the librarian select books when she is ordering annual library additions. A school that we worked with did this and found that the number of books checked out by the boys went up significantly when they had input into the choices. The committee

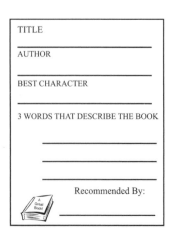

TITLE

AUTHOR

BEST CHARACTER

3 WORDS THAT DESCRIBE THE BOOK

Recommended By:

members had to research the books they were recommending and convince the committee to include their books on the list submitted to the librarian.

Next, talk to fellow teachers at your school: What books have been a real hit with their boys or their girls? Be sure that teachers indicate whether the book appealed to one sex more than the other or to both. That will start a rich discussion among teachers about books and authors, along with all the reasons that a particular book is so beloved.

Here are a few other resources that can help you to find great new books for your classroom and library:

What Stories Does My Son Need: A Guide to Books and Movies That Build Character in Boys, by Michael Gurian (Tarcher, 2000)

Great Books for Boys: More than 600 Books for Boys, 2 to 14, by Kathleen O'Dean (Ballantine, 1998)

Great Books for Girls: More Than 600 Books to Inspire Today's Girls and Tomorrow's Women, by Kathleen O'Dean (Ballantine, 1997)

The Kingfisher Book of Great Boy Stories: A Treasury of Classics from Children's Literature, by Michael Morpurgo (Kingfisher, 2000)

100 Books for Girls to Grow On, by Shireen Dodson (Harper, 1998)

Girls Who Rocked the World: Heroines from Sacagawea to Sheryl Swoopes, by Amelie Welden (Beyond Words, 1998)

Girls Who Rocked the World 2: Heroines from Harriet Tubman to Mia Hamm, by Amelie Welden (Beyond Words, 2000)

The Kingfisher Book of Great Girl Stories: A Treasury of Classics from Children's Literature, by Rosemary Sandberg (Kingfisher, 1999)

Boys Who Rocked the World: From King Tut to Tiger Woods, by Lar DeSouza (Beyond Words, 2001)

Canadian Boys Who Rocked the World, by Tanya Lloyd Kyi and Simon Jackson (Beyond Words, 2007)

Integrating Reading and Technology for Girls

Other initiatives around the country have tapped into the needs and interests of girls. One such program, *Read n' Rap,* is an innovative program that integrates reading and technology. Girls in fourth, fifth, or sixth grade are paired with high school girls to read and discuss novels via e-mail. Students at Muscatine High School and Franklin, McKinley, and Mulberry elementary schools in Iowa pioneered this program in 1998–99. In succeeding years the word spread, and several more elementary and middle schools joined the program. Through a serendipitous connection, elementary education students at the University of Northern Iowa also became involved.

Check It Out: Guys Read

Guys Read (www.guysread.com) is a Web site developed by children's book author Jon Scieszka. The mission of Guys Read is "to motivate boys to read by connecting them with materials they will want to read, in ways they like to read." The following is the Guys Read mission statements:

1. Make some noise for boys. We have literacy programs for adults and families. GUYS READ is our chance to call attention to boys' literacy.

2. Expand our definition of reading. Include boy-friendly nonfiction, humor, comics, graphic novels, action-adventure, magazines, Web sites, and newspapers in school reading. Let boys know that all these materials count as reading.

3. Give boys choice. Motivate guys to want to read by letting them choose texts they will enjoy. Find out what they want. Let them choose from a new, wider range of reading.

4. Encourage male role models. Men have to step up as role models of literacy. What we do is more important than all we might say.

5. Be realistic. Start small. Boys aren't believing that "Reading is wonderful." Reading is often difficult and boring for them. Let's start with, "Here is one book/magazine/text you might like."

6. Spread the GUYS READ word. Encourage people to use the information and downloads on this site to set up their own chapters of GUYS READ, and get people thinking about boys and reading.

Used by permission from Guys Read. © Jon Scieszka.

The project is coordinated by Mississippi Bend Area Education Agency, a regional service agency.

The girls read books chosen from a list selected by their teachers. The novels all feature strong female main characters and are at an appropriate reading and interest level for the younger girls. Historical and contemporary fiction and biographies are among the choices. While reading a particular book, the partners discuss the book and their reactions to it via e-mail.

Some schools allow the use of free Web-based e-mail accounts, while others elect to have all mail sent to the teacher's e-mail address. A moderated listserv is used to monitor the correspondence.

You can do all or part of what is being done in these schools in your own school or district, especially if you team up with other teachers—and with students themselves!

Giving Students Gender Choice in Reading and Writing: Is It Stereotyping?

In research conducted by Shelley Peterson at the University of Toronto, students in grades four and eight said that girls could write about almost anything, including topics that were viewed as "boy topics," whereas boys had to avoid typically feminine topics such as romance and other relationship-oriented writing in order to avoid peer ridicule. Thomas Newkirk in *Misreading Masculinity* points out that girls have social permission to write about their feelings and express affection. Boys, however, are different. Boys are apt to write action stories filled with danger and violence, in which the characters go through an exciting experience together and triumph.

The 2003 Canadian Adolescent Boys and Literacy Study, as well as studies done in Australia and the United Kingdom between 1994 and 1998, showed that boys are faced with many contradictions between school literacy practices and societal expectations regarding masculinity. These studies report that one social resistance to literacy is rooted in the belief that reading and writing aren't appropriately masculine.

As reported in *Boys and Girls Learn Differently!*, "Pecking orders (social strata) are very important to boys; they are often fragile learners when they are low in the pecking order." With a natural desire to "fit in," boys may gravitate to topics considered more masculine, or may turn away from reading. When they gravitate toward aggression-oriented themes, violence, slapstick humor, being gross, and so on, we teachers often overreact, thus barring from the classroom what the boys enjoy.

What do we do with the gender conundrums that human nature and human socialization have created for us? One thing we can do is listen in our own schools to conversations our kids are having. This informal study, completed in Colorado, with elementary-age boys and girls, yielded a fairly predictable list of favorite writing topics. You can take an informal survey of your students. It can become a class project, part of your language arts curriculum.

Topics Favored by GIRLS:	**Topics Favored by BOYS:**
Fairies, trolls, leprechauns	Football, any sport
Animals	Funny or scary stories
Holidays	Hunting
Stuffed animals	Chocolate monsters
Dolphins	Hurricanes, tornadoes, black holes
Poems	Hot Rods, sports cars
Family	Army stuff

Different times in my life	Robots
Dancing	Halloween
Mermaids	Adventures and mysteries
Best friends	How to get to the next level on a video game

Upon seeing the results of this survey, one teacher said, "This is all just stereotypes. We have to get the kids away from this stuff." While too much of any one thing can limit a child, there is another way to look at this survey. As another teacher said, "If this is what they like, what's wrong with it? There's nothing wrong with any of this—it's just different."

The schools we have worked with enjoy the debate on the politics of gender-specific imagery; at the same time, individual teachers almost always end up finding success in improving literacy by following choice making and novelty in the child's school day. They find that expanding girls' and boys' choices beyond stereotypes is a wonderful thing—keeping in mind that some of what girls and boys are trying to do is not stereotypical. It is primal, deep within the brain, and reading and writing needs to reflect this reality.

On pp. 77 and 78 are two interesting examples.

A Word About Violence

It can be hard to know where to draw the line when considering violence in students' writing. Certainly, in this era of school shootings, we need to be cognizant of "warning signs" in writing. Our research shows that at the elementary level, violence in writing rarely means that a plausible threat exists. If we've got a student enthusiastically writing (especially a typically reluctant student!), we certainly don't want to squeeze the motivation out of him! At the same time, good writers have a calling: they need to consider their reader. Talk to all of your students about the "audience" for each of their writing pieces. If the piece is too violent to be read by the audience, the writer has not done his or her job.

- Is this a private piece that won't be shared beyond the teacher?
- Will this piece be shared with students in the class?
- Will it be shared with younger students?
- How will this piece affect the readers?
- Is the content of the piece appropriate for this audience?
- Would it be rated "G" or "PG"?

Love

freind ship, a kiss from a
mother, a hug from a father,
a laygh from a child, a
song long and low, a lulaby
sang only from the heart, a
thanks giveing meal, This makes
one word... LOVE!

to! Mrs. Gipson
from! Alyssa

Written by third grader Alyssa, this piece is a good example of a female student's willingness to write about emotions. The emphasis is on feelings.

These questions are a good way to guide your students appropriately without telling them that they *can't* or *shouldn't* write about certain topics. They answer the questions and make their own choice—if they know from answers to these questions that their piece really is too violent, but they write it that way anyway, then their grade will drop accordingly. They choose, they suffer the consequences.

With time, your student writers will develop the maturity to be more independent in considering the audience for each piece that they write.

This piece, written by second grader Jackson, gives us a peek at this boy's experimentation with a "gross" topic in his writing. Note how he has illustrated his "frozen nose droppings."

It Was So Cold
By Jackson

It was so cold that the earth cracked and my breath turned to ice. I could use my nose droppings like a pair of chopsticks. It was so cold the sun disappeared and it was below zero degrees. Even my eyes had goose bumps! I shook like a cowboy on a horse. It was so COLD!

Simultaneously, answering questions of audience reception can help both boys and girls grapple with complex issues such as aggression, giving them a safe venue—their writing—in which to push limits and explore their thoughts and emotions in a healthy way.

Writing to Prompts on State Assessments

All of us write better when we have a vested interest, passion, or emotional connection with the content. So, how do we get passionate about a prompt on a state writing exam? Let's start by taking a look at a handful of released writing prompts from the grades 3–8 Colorado writing assessment (CSAP) in 2001–2004. As you read through these prompts, look for what these particular writing prompts have in common.

- What makes you happy? Describe what makes you happy and explain why.

- Explain what is most important to you in a friendship.

- Tell about a time when you felt good because you helped someone.

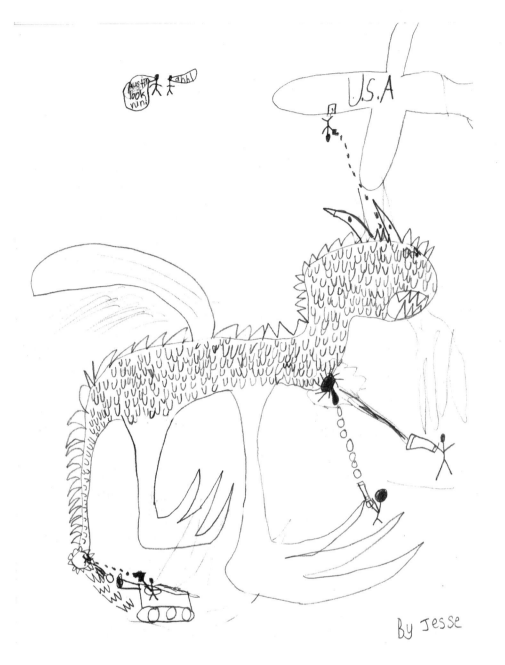

This boy's pre-writing drawing is full of action, conflict, and violent themes.

- If you could change just one thing about the world, what would it be?

- Write a well-developed paragraph giving advice about sixth grade to your friend.

- Think about a special person in your life. Compose a piece of writing in which you explain the impact that person has had on your life.

- Write a paragraph in which you describe your favorite season of the year and tell why it is your favorite.

- Many famous people, both real and fictional, have been honored by having their pictures on postage stamps. Choose a real or fictional person whom you feel deserves this honor.

- Write an essay in which you explain the impact that certain words have had on you.

- Think of something important you have that you did not buy. Write an explanation telling its importance to you.

What strikes you as you read these prompts? Generally speaking, who do you think would be more interested in writing about these topics—boys or girls? Why is that? Look back at the prompts again and think about whether the prompts ask students to write about *feelings* or *actions.*

In *Boys and Girls Learn Differently: An Action Guide for Teachers,* Gurian and Ballew explain the brain-based differences in the processing of emotion between boys and girls. "The female brain processes more emotive stimulants, through more senses, and more completely than does the male. It also verbalizes emotive information quickly . . . more of her activity moves up to the hemispheres that verbalize and reason." On the other hand, the male's ". . . emotive processing takes longer and involves less reasoning." Both the differences in boys' and girls' emotional processing and their interests affect their approach to—and ultimately their success with—prompt writing.

Of course, we've already determined that boys have a strong preference for writing about actions and doing over feelings and emotions. Many girls do as well. The last thing we want to do is to have our students take their state tests with one arm tied behind their backs, so to speak. But if we can't change the prompt, what can we do? We need to help our kids find something in those prompts that they can run with—while staying on topic, of course. So let's take another look at a few of the prompts. We've paired them with suggestions for writing to the prompt that may spark students' interests and that incorporate more action.

- What makes you happy? Describe what makes you happy and explain why.

    Write about what you love to do—play in a championship game, go hunting, get to the next level on a video game, win a race.

- Explain what is most important to you in a friendship.

    Instead of writing about a friend's personal qualities, consider writing about having shared interests in the same sports or activities, such as hockey, soccer, hunting, etc.

- Think about a special person in your life. Compose a piece of writing in which you explain the impact that person has had on your life.

    Could this person be a parent, big brother, big sister, relative or a coach who helped you get really good at something you love to do?

- Write a paragraph in which you describe your favorite season of the year and tell why it is your favorite.

  > Pick a season based on what you love to DO during that season—Baseball? Swimming? Watch football? Dress up for Halloween?

Try making this an exercise in your classroom, especially in the test-taking grades, to practice with "really boring" writing prompts: Have the kids make up some of the worst prompts they can think of! Make them gender-friendly for both boys and girls. Then work together as a class to figure out how to take such prompts and turn them into something that the students can care about. This activity will help both boys and girls be better equipped to channel their own interests into their prompt writing when test taking time comes along.

Common Teacher Questions and Concerns

I don't have time to cover the curriculum as it is. How do I incorporate what students want to read and write about?

There are certainly times when you can offer more choice and other times when you need to direct the content with less opportunity for choice. In these latter cases, there are still ways to let students "make it their own." While they may not have chosen to study the Civil War (or whatever topic you need to teach), is there a way to engage them that might make them change their minds? Or, might there be a way to help them approach the learning with more enthusiasm than they might have otherwise mustered?

Jeff Wilhelm, in *Action Strategies for Deepening Comprehension*, gives a great example of how he engages students prior to teaching a piece of literature. In order for the students to personalize the conflict in the story, Jeff has his students identify themselves as a New England Patriots fan or as a fan of the archrival New York Jets. He asks them to stand on opposite sides of the room and then interact as if they are on their way to the championship game. They prepare quickly and then taunt each other, make gestures, such as thumbing their noses, in a good-natured way. With their energy levels high, he refers them back to the characters involved in the conflict in the story. In Jeff's class, they are studying *Romeo and Juliet*, but the scenario can be applied to the Loyalists and the Tories, the Unionists and the Confederates or any content area in which conflict is the theme. In this situation, the students do not get to *choose* whether or not they study the lesson of the day or week, but their attention and motivation centers are definitely activated in regards to the topic.

Another way to integrate choice making into a lesson the students have not chosen is to focus not only on content, but also on process and product. Sometimes, you can't adjust the content (the "what" of your teaching), but you can consider ways to offer choice in the process ("how" students learn the information) and the product ("how" students demonstrate their knowledge). Can they research on the Internet? Can they interview people? Can they work in interest centers or develop their own study proposals? What are the options for assessments and culminating projects? Be sure to check out Chapter Seven, "Get Real," for more detailed information on ideas for giving students choice in the processes and products of learning.

What if I have students who only want to read comic books?

For some children, parameters may need to be established. It does not improve literacy to have them only read comic books all day. Hopefully, however, you can establish a system for planned reading and choice reading that shows them a process of give and take in place.

What we want to do is "legitimize" the forms of literature that they enjoy and use in their lives outside of school, even those that have historically been considered nonschool forms of literacy. Telling students that what they like to read "doesn't count" doesn't help them to develop a positive attitude towards reading—and when we ask them to read something challenging or less interesting to them, we definitely need them to have a positive attitude.

What will work in your classroom will depend on a lot of different variables, including the students' ages. If you give students independent reading time in class, consider designating half of the time as free choice reading. The other half of the time, have them read something that you've both had a hand in choosing, even comic books.

It is good to remember, as we end this dialogue on reading choice, that when students are given assigned reading and asked to read on their own, the reluctant or struggling readers often learn to "fake read." You can decrease the chances of this by making sure that the reading material for each child is fairly easy to read. Independent reading time can also be a great time to employ parent volunteers or older students to check-in with students about what they're reading. Talking to students about their free choice reading allows you to demonstrate interest in and understanding of the child's personal interests, and it compels the student to report what he or she has read—it's hard to fake it anymore!—even if the reading is a comic book.

WRAPPING UP THE MAIN IDEAS

- Increasing students' attention and motivation for learning by offering more choice increases students' learning, success, and confidence.

- Ensure that your classroom library is well-stocked with traditional "school" reading materials, as well as "nonschool" types of reading materials.

- Take into consideration students' personal interests outside of school and student book recommendations when purchasing new books for your classroom.

- Allow students opportunities to write about what they want to write about. Generally, at the elementary school level, you don't need to make many topics off limits.

- Become more accepting of student writing that is gross, violent, edgy, or silly.

- Teach students strategies for becoming more invested in writing in response to prompts on tests.

Get Them Learning Together

Increasing Opportunities for Social Interaction

5

Individually, we are one drop. Together, we are an ocean.
—Ryunosuke Satoro

MOST children report that "seeing my friends" is one of the main reasons they enjoy coming to school. Humans are social creatures and, for most, interacting socially—whether with one close friend or a wide circle of friends—is enjoyable. Social interaction can be a great motivator for students, and definitely a great teacher. It can also make or break a student. Social competence is the single best predictor of behavioral success in adulthood. Students who display antisocial behavior—such as difficulty regulating emotions, maintaining close friendships, or acting aggressively—are at greater risk of dropping out of school or developing mental health problems later in life.

How do we harness the appeal and power of social interaction to enhance motivation and to teach important skills? Let's look carefully at this now.

Why Social Interaction Works

The inventor and entrepreneur Henry Ford once said, "If everyone is moving forward together, then success takes care of itself." These are wise words for children's development.

In collaboration with one another, students solve problems, present and consider differing points of view, review prior knowledge, develop new strategies, share ideas, "think out loud" as they work through issues, brainstorm, debate, organize their thinking, develop empathy, shift points-of-view, hone questioning skills, and expand their understanding of the world. All of this

---

?

DID YOU KNOW? Social Skills Make A Difference In Learning!

Studies show that increasing social skills can help students in the following ways

- Increased achievement

- Reduction in risk behaviors

- Positive school culture committed to learning

- Less social isolation of students

- Increased creativity and problem solving

- Decreased level of stress

- Increased resilience

---

happens because the brain learns well within the comfort and challenge of social interaction. The experience of social interaction in the classroom will reenergize the brain, enhance focus, and will typically incorporate some kind of movement opportunities.

This occurs because social connections provide the learning brain with the kind of stimulation that translates into intrinsic motivation for engagement. Learning independently can of course be a powerful way to learn (solitude has its own intrinsic learning value), but for the developing brains of elementary school children, being social generally involves getting more active, getting out of one's seat, interacting with others and, in the minds of students, having more fun. These kids learn in *dialogic interactions* through which they engage the world. These dialogic interactions can motivate all kids, and can be especially helpful to those boys and some girls for whom sitting and listening to the teacher is more apt to lead to a neural rest state—the "zone out" mode.

In her work with seventh and eighth graders, teacher Joanna Hawkins paid careful attention to the dialogic interactions in her class and found that building working knowledge of a topic included frequent, intentional use of social interaction. Some of the interaction was physical, spatial, and kinesthetic—the boys seemed to need more of this—and much of it was also guided oral conversation. Through this interaction, fragmented knowledge was transformed into real understanding. This doesn't start in middle school. It must begin in the elementary years.

In *Reading Don't Fix No Chevys*, Smith and Wilhelm report that being social was very important to the boys in their study. "[T]he boys talked about the social in a variety of ways: how friends and family affected literate interests; the importance of relationships with teachers; their enjoyment of working in groups; and the importance of relationships they cultivated with textual characters, authors, or directors."

Other recent research offers compelling evidence that discussion-based learning leads to powerful learning, particularly when abetted by curricular cohesion and an emphasis on high academic achievement. Research from the American Association of Women showed through the 1990s how crucial it is to engage girls in classroom discussions. They learned better when they were invited to be a crucial part of the social interaction of the classroom.

When Sense of Safety Goes Up, So Does Learning

The human brain is constantly engaging and working—processing learning and life experience by creating internal hierarchies of tasks (of course, some hierarchies are imposed by parents, teachers, and the world). The brain's task hierarchy will start with physical survival, then move into emotional survival; once these feel accomplished by the brain, it moves into acuity in thinking and learning. Can a brain learn when under physical and emotional stress? Yes, it can, but until these stressors are dealt with, it will not learn much more than what is required for the survival mechanisms.

Well-organized (and comfortably spontaneous) social interactions in the classroom create an atmosphere of mutual trust and support that decrease the likelihood of the brain releasing the powerful stress hormone cortisol, which tends to keep the child focused on physical and emotional stress, rather than on higher learning. Researchers from the University of Georgia and San Diego State University report that social exclusion actually causes changes in brain function and can lead to poor decision making and a diminished learning ability. "Our findings indicate that social rejection can be a powerful influence on how people act," said W. Keith Campbell, a psychologist who led the research.

This new research is the first to examine subjects' brain patterns following social exclusion using the magnetoencephalography (MEG) technique. The MEG data revealed that those in the social-exclusion group had clear differences in activity in the brain's occipital, parietal, and prefrontal cortex regions. The inference is that social exclusion actually affects the brain's neural circuitry. "We found that there was a direct link between social exclusion, brain activity, and performance," said Campbell. Research has also shown that girls who are excluded socially can perform adequately in the classroom, while boys who are low in the social order tend to perform more poorly. This doesn't mean that the girls are not suffering from social rejection—it just means that they are still able to succeed academically.

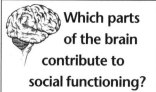

Which parts of the brain contribute to social functioning?

Social functioning requires a complex exchange of information between the outside world and the brain. The brain engages all of its lobes to take in information, access prior experience, process emotion, formulate language, and plan responses.

Frontal lobe: organizes and arranges information; coordinates planning, problem solving, judgment, the production of language, and the focusing of attention

Parietal lobe: process sensory data and plays a part in language

Occipital lobe: processes visual input

Temporal lobe: responsible for hearing, senses, language, learning and parts of memory

Limbic system: connected structures in this midbrain area are involved in emotional response, including the hypothalamus, amygdala, thalamus, fornix, hippocampus, and cingulate gyrus

Broca's area: responsible for oral language production

Wernicke's area: responsible for language comprehension

The implications of this for the classroom are not new to you as a teacher, but they definitely bear conscious planning. Many of the activities in this chapter are easy-to-use ways of getting your students interacting through team building. Once students have established personal relationships with one another and a sense of mutual trust, they feel safe to take risks inherent with new learning. They're ready to work together in meaningful and significant ways to support one another's learning. This team building isn't always a matter of using words, and it might not necessarily look the same, all the time, for boys and girls.

SOMETHING TO THINK ABOUT: DIFFERENCES IN GROUP LEARNING EXPERIENCES

Excerpt from *A Fine Young Man: What Parents, Mentors and Educators Can Do to Shape Adolescent Boys into Exceptional Men* by Michael Gurian.

Girls gravitate more easily to small group learning experiences than boys. By this we mean they will tend to move to a small group learning experience by self-motivation, whereas boys will tend to have to be directed toward it. Once in the group, girls will spend less time than boys making administrative decisions (sometimes they won't make them), e.g., who's going to lead.

A lot is hidden in this activity: the male push toward personal performance and pecking orders, the male push toward independent action and gain. This is not to say males are not team-oriented. Of course they are, but in many ways they tend toward larger group teams than females do—hunting groups, large work groups, sports teams. In the arena of learning, we find males holding back a little more than females when it comes to teaming up in small groups.

Focusing on Team Building in Your Class

Andrew Carnegie said, "Teamwork is the ability to work together toward a common vision. It is the fuel that allows common people to attain uncommon results."

Daniel Goleman calls this ability to relate to others "emotional intelligence," and has shown through his research that the skills of self-awareness, mood-management, motivation, empathy, and interpersonal skills can be learned in teams. According to Goleman, students learn

Self-awareness: knowing one's emotions, recognizing feelings as they occur, and discriminating between them

Mood management: handling feelings so they're relevant to the current situation

Self-motivation: "gathering up" feelings and directing oneself towards a goal, despite self-doubt, inertia, and impulsiveness

Empathy: recognizing feelings in others and tuning into their verbal and nonverbal cues

Managing relationships: handling interpersonal interaction, conflict resolution, and negotiations

In creating a successful team atmosphere for building emotional intelligence in your classroom, it is important to begin with an awareness of the *characteristics of a team* and the *benefits of teamwork.* You can work with your students first to see what they already know about teams and teamwork before supplementing their thinking with the research. They'll never know they are developing "emotional intelligence," but they will be doing so.

Teacher Terry Macauley asks his fifth graders if they know what the characteristics of a team are. He carries on this discussion in the first days of class. He asks students what they think are the characteristics of a team, the benefits of team building, the rules that should be set. He also teaches his students what they may be unable to articulate.

Characteristics of a Team:

- All team members must be aware of a sense of unity.

- There must be interpersonal relationships.

- Members must give one another a chance to contribute, learn from, and work with others.

- Members can argue and disagree, but then must come together to gain the ability to act together toward a common goal.

Benefits of Team Building:

- **Perseverance.** It is important for students to understand that success doesn't always come easy. Failure only means the need to try again or to re-think strategies. The wonderful line from the movie "Batman Begins" can be used by students with each other when a student fails: "Why do we fall, Bruce? To pick ourselves back up again."

- **Rules.** In team building there must be clear rules that are followed and if they are not then consequences result. Whether the rules are for a game or for expected behaviors, they must be set up to promote respect, responsibility, and safety but at the same time they must be open enough to allow for student creativity, exploration, and experimentation.

- **Social Development.** It is important to remember in team building that the main objective is not always to quickly solve a problem, but sometimes to see how the group works together to try to complete the task at hand.

TEACHING HINTS FOR TEAM BUILDING

1. Remember that safety is always the first concern. Make sure rules are clear about appropriate uses for equipment and the expected behavior for each challenge.

2. Keep in mind that the main goal of team building is for students to work together and support one another (it is not always how fast you can complete the challenge). This means positive comments only and definitely no put-downs toward others.

3. Team building should stress cooperation over competition, but making it clear that competition is not always a bad thing.

4. Most team-building activities can be modified to fit students of all ages and abilities. Changing the rules, equipment, or distances can make a big difference in the challenge (to make it easier or harder depending on your students' abilities).

5. Praise students when you see examples of positive life skills, cooperation, or sportsmanship. You can even award points in many of the games based solely on positive behavior or words. This will help reinforce those positive behaviors in your class.

6. As a teacher you want to make sure that you don't solve the challenges for the students. It is important that they work together and even struggle together to take on a challenge. Exceptions to this apply if the students are struggling in ways that can't be resolved by them—then you can modify the activity or give little hints. The key here is not to make it so easy that they don't have to think for themselves.

7. One of the best parts of team-building activities is the discussions that can follow up a group challenge. Some good questions to ask your students after participating in a team building activity include:

   a. What worked well?

   b. What did not work well?

   c. Was the group successful? Why or why not?

   d. What would you do different if you could try it again?

Source: Zack Dee, Petaluma Junior High

Social interaction is sometimes about product, but sometimes about process. Indeed, for young learners, the process can be the product.

Practical Ideas for Your Classroom

Fourth-grade teacher Sara Washington said this about the social interactions in her class: "There are so many benefits to having teams in my class, I can hardly begin to name them. Teamwork helps the boys learn how to deal with their feelings, it helps the girls find their voices, it helps all the kids learn. It allows for some healthy competition, which resonates for the boys more naturally but is really good for preparing girls for life. It also shows kids what the real world will be like—learning and living will be a team effort. Some teachers are lecturers—they themselves don't spend much time in teams and so they don't use teams to teach. They think their job will be harder if they have to build teams. I've found that teaching is easier. The kids are learning not just from me but from each other. They learn more and achieve more because they keep each other motivated."

Sara's experience—and her assessment of others' experiences in her school—seems to resonate with many teachers. If teams and social interactions are working well, kids will learn from one another in ways and amounts one teacher cannot ensure.

Here are now a number of practical suggestions for improving and utilizing social interactions and team efforts in your classroom.

Reading in Literature Circles

A *literature circle* is a structure for getting students to talk about a novel with their peers as they read it together. In literature circles, students are actively engaged in reading through making choices, discussing, and constructing meaning. This strategy engages students in higher-level thinking and reflection by encouraging collaboration and constructing meaning with other readers.

Various versions of book clubs and literature study circles have been found to increase student enjoyment of and engagement in reading; to expand children's discourse opportunities; to increase multicultural awareness; to promote other perspectives on social issues; to provide social outlets for students; and to promote gender equity.

Typically, there are between four to six students in a literature circle, and each member rotates through various "jobs" during the course of the group. Janet Lopez, a teacher at Dzantik'I Heeni Middle School in Juneau, Alaska, reports: "The students really love the approach because they are empowered with so much choice and get to 'run' the show." A fifth grader who participates in literature circles reports: "It's cool to be able to switch roles. Sometimes, I imagine a character one way but then someone draws the character a completely different way. We get to see what other people think about the book."

Although the terminology used to name the different "jobs" or roles in a literature circle may vary, they usually fall along these lines:

The Artist: uses some form of artwork to represent a significant scene or idea from the reading.

The Word Watcher: points out interesting or important passages within the reading.

The Discussion Leader: writes questions that will lead to discussion by the group.

The Real World Connector: finds connections between the reading material and something outside the text, such as a personal experience, a topic studied in another class, or a different work of literature.

The Dictionary Diver: discusses words in the text that are unusual, interesting, or difficult to understand.

Fourth-grade teacher Linda McCarthy finds it helpful to teach all of her parent volunteers about the different literature circle roles so that they can support the students during the circles. A list of the roles and responsibilities is kept in the parent volunteer folder for their reference. The parent volunteer supports the flow of the discussion and ensures that the roles are rotated and assigned for the next group meeting. When, as time goes by, student groups often learn to facilitate their own discussions—independent of constant adult supervision and guidance—the parent volunteers can become less directive.

To initiate literature circles in your own classroom, start by assessing the discussion skills of your students.

- Get learners involved in this process by brainstorming lists of the qualities of "effective" and "ineffective" group participation. What does a good listener do or not do?

- Teach some basic discussion etiquette. Try some role playing and modeling using a read-aloud book. Practice these techniques in small groups.

- Debrief the group using reflection techniques such as asking them to recall something that went poorly or particularly well.

- Help students create a set of discussion guidelines that can serve as reminders.

- Periodically provide ideas for ways the groups can strengthen their discussion skills.

- Try some gender-specific literature circles and observe any difference between those and coed groupings.

As students learn how to work together in a literature circle, they will be engaging in enthusiastic, natural and informative conversations about their reading. Ultimately, the social interactivity of literature circles will stimulate neurological activity that is conducive to learning, put learning within an emotional context, hone students' interpersonal skills, increase engagement in and motivation for the text, and better teach the content.

Using Study Groups

Student study groups differ somewhat from literature circles. If the purpose of a literature circle is to understand a text more deeply, a study group is charged with reading, writing, and thinking critically about a topic—and moving toward some kind of action. Study groups may work to solve a real-world problem for which a solution has not yet been developed. The group might help design a new playground, analyze the amount of waste in the cafeteria each day and institute a recycling program, analyze current events and write legislators, or interview war veterans and create historical fiction based on their stories. Again, trying a variety of study group designs may be useful; gender-specific and coed groupings may result in different kinds of interactions and insights into students' attitudes about reading material.

For more on working in your classroom and study group on problems that are meaningful, realistic, and authentic, see Chapter Six, "Making It Real!"

Using Vertical Mentoring

Vertical mentoring is the process of allowing students from different grade levels to pair up for the purpose of interaction. Perhaps you have heard of vertical mentoring being referred to as "classroom buddies" or "multiage buddies." Note that vertical mentoring is also discussed in Chapter Eight, "Connecting with Your Students."

Studying wisdom-of-practice research on the merits of vertical mentoring, we can ascertain that this mentoring does two important things. First, the friendships that are formed help students to feel valued and cared for. This releases endorphins and dopamine—the neurotransmitters that make us feel good and enjoy our work more. Second, students can provide excellent social and academic feedback to one another. When students talk to other students, they get specific feedback on their ideas as well as their behaviors.

At Douglass Elementary School, Stephanie Buchan's fifth graders and Kathy Ransom's kindergartners buddy-up for a number of activities throughout the year. Stephanie reports that her fifth graders show an entirely different side of their personalities when they are nurturing and supporting younger children. Kathy shares, "The Kinders adore their buddies and exchange pleasantries, high-fives and hugs in the hall. The fifth graders have helped the Kinders integrate into the family spirit of our school."

Indeed, in your own school, you'll find that children are motivated by the opportunity to share something that they've created with an older student. Having a "buddy" provides an audience for one's work. When an older student is writing for a younger student, he or she typically wants to make sure that the story is well illustrated and neatly printed so as to be

TEACHERS TALKING

Second-grade teacher Mary Jo Barbeau and fourth-grade teacher Lynn Twietmeyer have partnered their classes for years. They share the following about the kinds of activities that their two classes have enjoyed:

Games: These are usually physical and outside. We found kids bond best by playing a game and having a common goal. We often use this as a way to discuss what works best and what does not work well when trying to reach a goal with a group of people. We usually do about two meetings this way to get us up and going. It is by far the best icebreaker we have found.

Writing: We do a variety of writing activities. We generally weave in character assets. We have done "poetry for two voices," similarities and differences pieces between the buddies, and a variety of other pieces.

Community service: Every spring, we go to a nursing home and do a musical presentation for the residents. It has been a great way to have the kids directly involved with community service. We also send over decorations throughout the year to encourage kindness and empathy.

Unit projects: Every year we have a project that fits in with a particular unit of study, generally the second-grade curriculum. The kids research the topic and then create a display.

Field trips: In the spring, we go on a field trip—usually a hike. The past few years we have hooked up with the city parks system and had volunteers teach us about outdoor safety and other relevant topics.

enjoyed by the younger child. When the younger child is doing the writing, she puts in more effort in order to impress the older child and be seen as competent in the older child's eyes.

If you haven't already partnered with a classroom at another grade level, ask around to see if there's another interested teacher. To the degree possible, pair up boys with boys and girls with girls. This allows for gender-specific nurturing systems (support *by* males *for* males and support *by* females *for* females) to be in place. Classroom buddies meet as often as arranged by the cooperating teachers and can share in a number of activities, including

- Partner reading

- Shared writing

- Working on a project or craft

- Corresponding with pen pals
- Community service
- Field trip
- Doing research
- Playing board games
- Team-building activities
- Class parties or celebrations

Classroom buddies creates a sense of community within our school. My second graders LOVE to have time with their buddies. Older students provide leadership by example and the time we have together provides us with an opportunity to do community service.
                    —Mary Jo Barbeau, second-grade teacher

Activities You Can Use Immediately

The following are a list of team-building games and cooperative learning activities designed to help students get to know one another, increase communication and collaboration, improve classroom climate, and enhance student learning.

In addition to creating opportunities for social interaction, these activities make great "brain-breaks" as discussed in greater detail in Chapter Two, "Keep 'Em Moving."

Meet Three People   Have students stand and shake hands with three people who . . . are wearing black, were born in the same state, have traveled to Europe, have an older sibling, who were born in the same month, and so on.

Musical Groups   Play some energizing music. Have students move around the classroom. When the music stops, have them take a seat at the nearest table group. This is a fun way to mix up your students to get them working with a different group from time to time.

Telling Yarns   Give each child a piece of yarn, letting students decide how long their pieces should be. One by one, the students tell a story about themselves while wrapping their piece of yarn around their finger. They keep talking until the yarn has been wrapped all the way around one finger.

We're Different, We're Alike   Have students pair up. Give each of them a sheet of paper with a large Venn diagram on it. Have them discuss and then draw or write on the diagram to show ways that they are alike and different. Share with the class.

Part of a Group   Give each student five small squares of two-by-two-inch paper. Ask them to think of five different groups that they belong to, such as a sports team, a scout pack, a reading group, a family. Have them illustrate each group with a symbol, one per square of paper. For the reading group, the student may choose to draw a book on his square. Take all of the students' squares and group them on a large sheet of paper to show how many different groups there are and how many students belong to each kind of group.

Classroom Quilt   Give each student a white five-by-five-inch square of paper and a colored six-by-six-inch piece of paper. Have each child illustrate something that is important to or about him or her on the white paper. Mat it on the colored paper and then mount all of the matted squares on a piece of butcher paper together to form a "quilt" that depicts the classroom community.

Teamwork in Action   Have students get into small groups of three to five students to talk about situations in the last week when they observed people working as a team (such as at the grocery store, on the playground, at a sporting event). Have them describe what they observed. Discuss as a whole class and make note of the words used to describe how they people interacted in these situations—"helping each other," "working together," "cooperating," and so on. Together, develop a definition of teamwork that can be displayed in the classroom.

Build It   Put students in larger groups of six to eight. Give each group four boxes, a roll of masking tape, a pair of scissors, a ruler, and a pencil or pen. Instruct the teams to build a chair (or other functional item of your or their choosing) using the supplies they've been given. When time is up, have the teams share their planning, building and decision-making processes. "Try out" each others' creations.

I Have a Friend Who   Place one less chair (or place marker) than the number of people. One person standing says, for example, "I have a friend who wears white shoes." People wearing white shoes get up and switch chairs with each other. (You can't sit in the same chair you just sat in.) The person left standing (who has no chair) is the next leader. Other examples: I have a friend who loves to read; plays soccer; has a birthday in July.

Blob   Play in a large area with boundaries. One player starts as the "blob." When she tags someone, that person joins hands with her and they try to catch others together. When there are at least four in the blob, they can split into two blobs. This repeats until everyone is caught.

WRAPPING UP THE MAIN POINTS

- Social interaction promotes neurological activity that is beneficial for learning.

- Getting students engaged with one another allows them to learn and refine essential interpersonal skills.

- Students' ability to manage their emotions and get along with others are among the most accurate predictors of their future success in life.

- Students who feel emotionally and socially safe in the classroom environment are able to learn and retain more because of lower levels of cortisol and other physical stress responses.

- Team-building activities, cooperative learning, literature circles, study groups, and vertical mentoring are all excellent ways to encourage and develop positive social interaction in the classroom.

- And here's a bonus: Many activities that involve social interaction also give the body a much-needed opportunity to move!

Making It Matter

6

Finding Ways to Make Learning Real

I want to be a baseball player or a cook. I guess I need to learn how to sign autographs and write cookbooks.

—Ben, second grader

HAVE you ever heard students say, "Do we have to do this?" or "What does this have to do with anything?"

You've said it yourself at various times in your life. We all have.

Some things just have to be done. There is drudgery in everything noble, there is a surface experience to every deep experience. Chores are as important as fighting battles against dark lords. It would be unrealistic to try to make every single thing a child learns immediately relevant to some great mission in life.

At the same time, it goes counter to human nature when rote learning strays too far from a child's reality. Children are learning their life purpose everyday. They are trying to understand who they are and who they must be. They need a great deal of their learning to *matter*. When too much of it doesn't, they turn away from learning, lose motivation, and even seek their life purpose in distracted, painful, wasteful, dangerous things. More significantly, the brain will only pay ultimate attention to those things it decides do have relevance and meet a need.

As you explore this chapter, keep in mind for which of your students this chapter is most crucial. Some of the children in your class are willing to do almost any work simply because they are asked to do so, or simply to please. Girls, especially, with their biological imperative to maintain relationships, will comply because you ask them to. This chapter is for them—the work in it will help you excite them. But perhaps for them this chapter's content is not most urgent. You may find that urgency exists for the kids in your class who have difficulty learning when their learning

? DID YOU KNOW? Boys Often Have More Trouble with Issues of Relevance

Have you noticed that girls are often more likely than boys to "learn through pleasing the teacher?" Have you noticed that there are generally more boys in an elementary school classroom who feel "out of it" when it comes to learning that is disconnected from reality? The number of boys who become oppositional (or labeled "lazy") in learning, doing homework, and following through is generally larger than the number of girls doing so.

One reason lies in biochemistry. Oxytocin is a primary human bonding neurotransmitter and is found in higher quantities in the female brain than the male brain. Oxytocin is a primary reason why females—whether in the workplace or school—tend to be more willing to comply to please others. Males, with lower levels of oxytocin and higher amounts of the aggression chemical, testosterone, often have a lower threshold for making themselves malleable as learners. Socialization factors can add to this male-female difference.

Although relevance of material to real life is important for all kids, don't be surprised if you notice that males often need more buy-in to find relevance—whether at work, at home, or, when children, at school.

content matters not at all to their lives. Sometimes these kids are defiant, oppositional, or seemingly passive and placid, but not doing their homework and not engaging in class. More boys than girls in your class may well fit into this group. With the relationship imperative not as motivational, boys are sometimes harder to convince; they need to find a valid connection between what they are learning and their real world.

This chapter will help you to engage all your students emotionally in the process of learning. This kind of engagement is a linking of the learner's purpose in life with learning, and it can be another piece of the puzzle for success. Don't be surprised if it is one of the tools in your toolbox that helps your class do better on tests, lowers discipline referrals to the principal, and creates a more comfortable and peaceful classroom.

The philosophy and tools of engagement you'll find in this chapter grow from the idea and the wisdom of practice that kids want to learn—and they can learn—when they "earn" the meaning of their learning through real connections to real things.

Why It's Important to Make Learning Matter for All Kids

Mel Levine, author of *A Mind at a Time,* provides a wonderful outlook on what it means to engage an individual mind in real life learning.

It's been shown that the best way to learn how to read well is to read about something you know a lot about and feel passionate about.

One of the ways we can leverage skills is by continually pegging them to a child's affinities . . . If I were the principal of a school, I would establish a policy that every fourth grader picks a topic he's going to stick with. And at the end of three years, the student makes a series of formal presentations. In the meantime, he reads every book in the library on spiders, and he does three art projects and four science projects on spiders. When the family goes on vacation, they photograph spider webs. And at school when there's a spider in the boys' restroom, he's called in for a consultation. An awful lot of important skills can ride the coattails of your affinities with strengths, you begin to carve out a potential career.

Michael Gurian has called this "nurturing the nature of your child." Nurturing the child's inborn nature gives the child a sense of purpose in life, by both tapping into his or her natural talents and affinities, and connecting them to honorable work.

Realistically, in our current standards-based system, we may not have the latitude to "do spiders" for four years, but there is still an important point to learn: students can, if given the chance, identify and follow their personal strengths, talents, and interests toward success. Teaching in a classroom that tries to force students to practice "other people's strengths" can backfire. Especially in an elementary classroom, where more than 90 percent of teachers are likely female, it's important to spend time thinking about what both girls *and* boys are interested in and will enjoy reading about.

What parts of the brain are trying to find relevance?

- *Right ventrial striatum:* a part of the brain responsible for calculating risk and reward. This area of the brain helps people summon motivation for a task.

- *Oxytocin:* neurotransmitter that increases the desire to bond with and please others. Females have more oxytocin than males.

- *Angio-vasopressin:* neurotransmitter responsible for intermale aggression, territoriality, bonding, and persistence.

- *Limbic system:* a group of interconnected deep brain structures involved in emotional connectivity, motivation and behavior.

- *Left frontal lobe:* an area that exercises conscious control over one's thoughts to allow for focusing of attention, prioritizing, and problem solving.

- *Reticular activating system:* a group of cells at the base of the brain stem that serve as the control center for attentiveness, motivation, self-control, and processing and learning of information.

Focusing on Purposeful Teaching

As you look at your classroom and its lessons, start your own internal dialogue about relevance and purpose by picking just a few lessons in which you can engage the students in interesting, real-world questions that organize and drive the subject matter. This is *purposeful teaching*.

Consider the following important tenets of purposeful teaching:

- Content is connected to the student's real world whenever possible—if you aren't personally familiar with the real world of your opposite gender, spend some time learning about those interest areas.

- Teachers are cognizant of learning styles, including those related to gender.

- Students are respected as central to learning.

- Students have opportunities to design projects—give boys and girls a chance to work in single-gender groups to brainstorm project ideas and note any differences.

- Students know their responsibilities for creating a positive learning environment.

- Everyone gets called on (even the shy ones!).

- Students keep portfolios and receive feedback not only from teachers but also from other students on the relevance of their work—be sure to focus on the content of the portfolio and not the presentation, as there is likely to be a difference in how boys and girls design their materials.

- Just as they would in a workplace, students must plan, set goals, and even show off a little!

- A student's progress is assessed individually—as befits his or her natural talents—as well as a part of the group.

Purposeful teaching is implicitly about nurturing the individual child's nature—and helping that child discover his or her own passions, interests, and internal assets for self-nurturing. Kids need external assets in order to help them learn—standardized tests, teachers imposing lessons, parents making sure they do their homework—but they also need to be developing, over the course of the learning years, their own sense of relevance. Purposeful teaching never loses sight of this. It seeks the little self-reflective comments and "aha" moments when the student's eyes light up.

I think kids should learn how to write so they can do job applications, write essays at their jobs and do deliveries.
—Owen, fifth grader

Project-Based Learning

One "light-giving" way to increase the connection between students' interests and purpose, the school curriculum, and the demands and rewards of the real world is to allow students to pursue project-based learning opportunities.

Project-based learning switches the emphasis from teachers teaching students in small increments of information to students doing and learning through extended projects. Students are able to exercise some choice regarding the content, as well as the learning activities and processes. The project typically relates to a real-world problem, issue, or investigation.

A great way to get started in matching students' interests with the curriculum is to utilize a student interest survey. Using vertical mentoring to develop student interest surveys can be very helpful—both for your class and for the students doing the mentoring. They will be sharing their interests as they try to elicit the interests of the younger students. Try to match boys with boys and girls with girls during this activity and observe any differences in motivation for students you are most concerned about.

What Is Project-Based Learning?

Project-based learning is a structure that transforms teaching from "teachers telling" to "students doing." More specifically, successful project-based learning

- Arises from a meaningful question

- Takes time

- Requires investigation

- Is semi-structured, requiring substantial student input

- Follows a timeline with articulated milestones to be reached along the way

- Requires a tangible end product

- Includes presentation for a real audience

- Includes moments of reflection

- Blurs subject area boundaries—emphasize issues, skills, and concepts

- Blurs the line between "slow" and "fast" learners

- Creates a culture of accomplishment in the classroom

- Connects students with adult mentors

- Conceives of teachers as "coaches" or "facilitators" and students as "workers"

With everything you have learned already about the differences in how boys and girls learn, look over the preceding list carefully. Make sure you are giving as much weight to the characteristics that might be more "boy friendly" or "girl friendly" as you evaluate projects. For instance, the ways in which girls and boys demonstrate "moments of reflection" might be quite different, but equally as successful.

Questions to Ask Yourself and Students:

- What questions or issues does the project address? How are they of real interest to the students and the larger community?

- What will students learn (academic content, knowledge, thinking skills)?

- How long will the project take, which adults will be involved, and what milestones will students reach along the way?

- What resources will students use for their investigation?

- What kind of ongoing support and feedback will students receive?

- What are the explicit expectations and criteria for success?

- How will students exhibit and present their project and what they have learned?

One great source of project-based learning opportunities is Future Problem Solving Program International. FPSP (www.fpsp.org) offers a year-long opportunity for teams of students to apply their problem-solving skills in their community through the "Community Problem Solving" challenge. In addition to studying their community problem, students plan a course of action and implement their plan. Teams move from hypothetical issues to real-world, authentic concerns and compete for an invitation to an international conference. Additionally, a year-long, non-competitive component called "Action-Based Problem Solving" is available and is designed for use in the regular classroom.

Social Action Projects

Children, even young children, can experience strong emotions when they see or learn of a problem in the world—whether it is pollution, homelessness, stray animals, loss of the rain forest, or bullying at their school. Emotions engage the attention and motivation of the individual and encourage people to take action. Just about any content area can have a natural tie to a social-action project. There are literally hundreds of different social-action projects in which your students might like to participate. Perhaps you can find something close to home, such as reducing waste at your school, designing playground improvements, or improving the school lunch program. If you and your students need some help finding worthwhile projects, check out these Web sites for ideas:

Do Something (www.dosomething.org/)

Do Something is a national non-profit organization that not only encourages young people to believe that change is possible but inspires them to be leaders who can implement change in their communities. It offers $500 grants to youth under thirty to implement service projects in their communities. The site has a grant application and information on obtaining sponsorship.

The Earth Day Project (www.earthdaybags.org/)

To celebrate Earth Day students decorate paper grocery bags with pro-environmental messages, and give them to stores to use to hold customers' groceries.

Explorers' Page (www.epa.gov/kids/)

This page has a lot of interesting information to develop projects about recycling, plants and animals, air pollution, and other environmental concerns.

Give Water a Hand (www.uwex.edu/erc/gwah/)

Teachers can download curriculum guides that will help classes perform service-learning projects with a focus on improving local water quality.

Kids Care Project (http://teams.lacoe.edu/documentation/projects/windows/care.html)

This project asks students to identify a community problem and develop an action plan, including writing persuasive letters to influential people to help combat the problem. Suggested topics include neighborhood cleanups, recycling, tree planting, and so on.

National Service-Learning Clearinghouse (www.servicelearning.org/)

The National Service-Learning Clearinghouse has lots of information for teachers of kindergarten through grade twelve to promote school-community connections through service projects.

Putting Kids in the Spotlight: Audience

Teachers at Douglass Elementary School asked themselves, "Why do writers want to write well?" We knew that some of the *adult* answers to that question were: to serve the reader well, to engage the reader, to be clear in our communications. For the kids, we found that a great motivator was to make sure they understood their obligation as writers to their audience. This is a crucial area of focus for any of the disciplines you are teaching. It can be handled through a number of lenses and approaches.

First might be to ask a child, "Who is the audience for this piece you've written?" The child may have difficulty answering the question, or may say "the teacher," "the class," or "my parents." If the piece is to be posted in the hallway, the student might say, "whomever walks by." If your students respond with any of these, they have taken a first step toward understanding the power of their audience to motivate them, but they may still not be tapping fully into that power. You may need to ask them to keep focused on one or more of the real-world readers. You may need to point out how some of their sentences just don't talk to that reader. It can be inspiring to a student to say, "You need more detail here in this paragraph to make sure your mother understands what you mean. Without giving the color of the shirt, or the color of the dog that crossed the road, or the kind of hat worn by the dog walker, your mom won't be able to see what you mean." This contextualizing of writing to a specific audience frees the mind to write better.

As you work with your students to help them focus on the audience for whom they are writing, again keep in mind that girls may tend to be more concerned about this issue as a result of their relationship orientation. Boys may tend to focus on their interest in the topic and less on the interest of their audience. It's important to not discourage the boys' enthusiasm; help them anticipate how they might motivate their audience to be interested in their topic, or how they can convince them. It can become a challenge and boys do love a challenge!

Here are some further ways to specifically focus both girls and boys on audience.

Vertical mentors: Classroom buddies, as they are typically called, are discussed in detail in Chapter Five, "Get Them Learning Together." Classroom buddies can be a wonderful audience for students' work. Generally, younger students are very motivated to write a better story or do their most fluent oral reading when they are sharing with an older student whom they admire or respect. They want to do a good job to impress their special friend. Older students usually feel a sense of obligation to do their best work for younger students because they want to create something nice to share and because it is important to appear competent. In both cases, the relationship between the two students creates a personal connection to the audience and, thereby, a greater sense of obligation to do one's best. For girls, their relationship imperatives will likely engage. For boys, their desire to lead from a step up the hierarchy may well kick in.

Publishing student work: There are a variety of mechanisms for publishing student work, including the traditional "publishing center" in classrooms or libraries, as well as a literary newspaper or journal that is printed periodically. When cost and environmental considerations are taken into consideration, it makes sense to make better use of technology. Why make the school community your audience when your audience can be the world? Student work is very easily posted on your school's Web site. It is helpful to find a parent volunteer who is willing to type or scan student work to go on the Web. (As students become more competent at keyboarding, let them prepare their own work!) When you consider the amount of time that it takes to lay out a literary magazine and the costs involved with printing it, you may wish to set up a "student work" link on your school's Web site and do most of your publishing there. Of course, make sure your students' distant family and friends know where to go online to see your students' work!

Podcasts: A fun application of technology is to create a simple Podcast for your school's Web site. You'll be amazed at how easy and fun it is! A Podcast is a digital audio recording that can be opened and played on a computer. It will require the purchase of a small digital recorder (approximately $50) with a built-in microphone. Alternately, it is possible to purchase a higher-quality external microphone. Use the digital recorder to record a student reading aloud his or her latest story. Plug the digital recorder into your computer via the USB port and save the audio file to your computer. The audio file can then be attached to an e-mail—just as a digital picture can—and sent anywhere you wish. The school webmaster can post your digital audio file on the Web site so that a worldwide audience can listen to your students read their stories or other projects aloud. Play the Podcast for your students and see how much fun it is for them to hear their own stories and to know that they can be heard all over the world!

School assemblies: Getting the entire student body and staff together in the gymnasium can create quite a substantial audience in most schools. Certainly, there is power to be harnessed from the motivation generated by knowing that dozens or hundreds of people will be listening. Perhaps you already have school assemblies for various functions or at regular intervals. Find ways to make these assemblies an audience opportunity for students!

At Douglass Elementary, a monthly all-school assembly is held to learn about one of the school's seven character assets. Each month, one class of students is asked to write original pieces about a particular character asset. Students eagerly and conscientiously seek out ways to make their pieces the best that they can be. At the assembly, they read or perform their pieces in groups or as individuals at microphones on a stage in front of five hundred people.

Additionally, the annual spring choir concert at Douglass Elementary has been turned into an "Arts Alive" program during which students' talents as singers, artists, and writers are showcased and celebrated. Prior to the music program, students do coffeehouse-type readings of their pieces in various rooms in the school. When the music program starts in the gym, it is interspersed with student readings of original pieces in front of a very large gathering. Musical selections are made to weave into the themes created by students' writing. The stage is decorated with students' artwork.

Teachers at Douglass knew that there were ways to give students an audience for their writing through existing assemblies and parent performances. Simply modifying programs already in place can be much easier than adding additional presentations and performances to an already busy calendar.

All willing eyes and ears: Most students value one-on-one time with an adult, and there is often very little of it available for students in the regular classroom. Take advantage of everyone in the building to sit down now and then and listen to a child's story, hear about a project, or admire the work. The principal, the secretary, the custodian, the assistant teacher, a parent volunteer—any of these folks could make a fine audience for a student. Let them know ahead of time how important it is for the students to have an opportunity to share their work one-on-one with an adult and coordinate a way to accomplish this. Remind the parents too. With their busy schedules, they may not realize or remember that it's important to stop and give one's attention fully to a child, especially when the child needs an audience for a wonderful piece of work. As often as possible, recruit male volunteers to work with boys. Adult males' showing an interest in a boy's academic performance can really help the boy see the value of education.

Once students have established an important and real audience for which they are obligated to do their best writing, it is helpful to teach students how to go about best considering the needs of their audience. Have students be very thoughtful in identifying both the purpose of their writing (see inset box in Chapter Three called "Eight Purposes of Writing"), as well as their audience.

Help students to answer the following questions about their audience so that they can make more informed decisions about how to approach the task of writing:

1. Who will read this?

2. What do they already know about my topic?

3. What do I want them to know?

4. What part of my topic would interest them most?

Using Competition to Help Build Relevance

In the last twenty years, classrooms have moved away from competition in favor of more collaborative and cooperative endeavors. In some cases, competition in the classroom has been completely eliminated. A total ban on competition is unfortunate and needs to be rethought. Competition is one of the very human ways in which children focus on and build their sense of purpose. Competition hones interests and passions, and competition compels a student to link his or her interests to paths of relevance. When there's no competition, it's much easier to focus on nothing of worth in particular—and do enough just to get by. Competition lead us to do more than that. For boys, competition ignites their testosterone-driven desire to compete. For girls, healthy competition can build self-confidence and willingness to take risks.

Cooperative learning is, of course, the norm for classrooms. Are targeted competition projects and activities contradictory to cooperation? They do not need to be. In our common parlance, we oppose competition with cooperation, but in real life, they are blended. People cooperate together to further a project; this cooperative group competes with another cooperative group. The different groups end up learning a great deal by having to compete with one another.

You may have noticed how energized some of your students are when you introduce competition into a project. Some kids might be uncomfortable and need close mentoring, but others will immediately pay closer attention, focus better on the learning, engage their emotions, and feel that the learning is more "real" now that it is competitive. Many teachers report that the boys in their classes will make a competition out of almost any activity they introduce, and as long as it remains positive, they don't mind since it provides added motivation.

Competition opportunities can be helpful for every student, and especially welcomed by boys who are listless in their learning. It can also be very valuable for young girls, who might not naturally compete enough in everyday life, to fully understand the need, in the future, to hon competition skills.

In the educational setting, we can achieve more or less healthy outcomes depending on how competition is applied. Any competition that becomes unhealthy will have the opposite effect of what we want—it can heighten stress so much that it interferes with learning.

If you decide to utilize more competition in your class, your goal will be to facilitate the kind of healthy competition that encourages students to put in extra time studying, preparing, and solving problems.

The ground rules for healthy competition include:

- It's for learning—not for creating a rivalry or cutting others down.
- All individuals or groups have a reasonable chance of winning.
- All of the students have a firm understanding of the first two points.

There are a number of competition opportunities available for students as both cocurricular and extracurricular pursuits. Here are some Web sites that our teachers have found most helpful:

Future Problem Solving (www.fpsp.org/)

Thinking Caps Quiz Bowl (www.thinkingcapquizbowl.com/)

Destination Imagination (www.idodi.org/)

National Geography Bee
(www.nationalgeographic.com/society/ngo/geobee/)

Scripps National Spelling Bee (www.spellingbee.com/about.asp)

Science Olympiad (www.soinc.org)

Ole Miss Problem of the Week
(www.olemiss.edu/mathed/problem.htm)

Practical Ideas for Your Classroom

Let's look together now at specific activities that you can use immediately in your classroom. As you review them, think about how the activity would be motivating for the boys in your class, and for the girls in your class.

Simulation Activities

Teacher Max Fischer, the author of a book of simulation activities for the social studies classroom, says: "When students are given an affective outlet in which their feelings are aroused to stimulate learning, we are increasing their opportunities to learn cognitively as well. . . . Simulations help deliver variety to my instruction and keep students engaged to the point that discipline rarely becomes an issue." In an *Education World* curriculum update article, Fischer shares one of his favorite simulation activities:

> After a number of years in teaching during which time I had used simulations sporadically at best, I created an activity that crystallized the engaging effects of a worthy simulation. I called it The King's M & M's. In order to get my students to realize how American colonists really felt about King George's Stamp Act and the subsequent Intolerable Acts, which taxed various imported goods such as tea, I gave each

student ten M&M's in a paper cup. I randomly assigned roles where most students were colonists, two were tax collectors, two were members of Parliament, and one was King George. Members of Parliament drew slips of paper out of a hat on which I had written down the names of some common items. These items—for example, blue jeans, Nike shoes, or eyeglasses—would be subject to taxation. The tax collectors came around and withdrew a specific number of candy pieces for each taxable item if a student possessed that item. The confiscated candies were distributed among Parliament members and the king (with a few going to the tax collectors). The student colonists were infuriated, and I compared their umbrage of the apparent inequity in candy distribution to what the colonists actually felt toward the British system of taxation. The fact that the students had no say in what was taxed in the classroom paralleled the infamous "taxation without representation" sentiment of the colonists.

What a wonderful real-world simulation. You can put this to work immediately.

Using Technology to Simulate the Real World

Education researchers are increasingly turning to computer and video games as tools for learning. Boys are often more easily engaged in learning when technology is involved, and it is helpful for girls to work more with technology to encourage them to explore many nontraditional careers. In the field of science, many educators advocate the notion that science concepts are best taught not by mathematical formulae, but rather through experiments, labs, demonstrations, and visualizations that help students engage with the physical phenomena in the real world.

At the same time, technologies can simulate the real world in their own unique way. By representing the simulation through digital gaming conventions, educators can increase even reluctant students' levels of engagement with the content and world.

In a Boston College study, researchers studied the effect of using a video game simulation to teach concepts related to electromagnetism. They found that "[f]or many students, but boys in particular, the point of the exercise was to beat the game, and the thought of replaying levels to try different strategies or learn about electromagnetism was uninteresting. For other students, many of whom were girls, the experience was less about beating the game and more about exploring the game simulation. These girls wanted to be able to record their actions, review levels, and share their results with peers."

What was learned from this study was that teachers need to maintain a high level of involvement during student-led simulations. In the case of the video game simulation on electromagnetism, the teacher created log sheets for students to record their actions and make predictions. This reinforced the purpose of the activity and encouraged students to detect patterns in their play. In addition, the teacher used the projector to display game levels, encouraging the class to interpret the events happening onscreen and make predictions about how they thought the simulation would behave. This structure added more focus to students' play and allowed the instructor to prompt deeper reflection on game play.

The Web site www.highsmith.com has some great published simulation materials you can incorporate into your classroom immediately. Check them out!

Tips for Successful Simulations

When using simulations, you might apply the following tips:

- If you are using a prepared simulation from a resource book, be sure to read it thoroughly and become familiar with the instructions. The first time with a simulation is always the most difficult.

- If a simulation is focused on creating a certain emotional response, be sure to debrief students before the end of the class period or the day. Be sure that they understand the relationship of the activity to the historical concept in the instructional objectives.

- Know your students well. Use your judgment about the appropriateness of simulations for your students, especially for those with any sort of emotional issues.

What are the traits of an essential question?

- The question probes a matter of considerable importance.

- The question requires movement beyond understanding and studying—some kind of action or resolve—pointing toward the settlement of a challenge, the making of a choice, or the forming of a decision.

- The question cannot be answered by a quick and simple "yes" or "no" answer.

- The question probably endures, shifts, and evolves with time and changing conditions—offering a moving target in some respects.

- The question may be unanswerable in the ultimate sense.

- The question may frustrate the researcher, may prove arid rather than fertile and may evade the quest for clarity and understanding.

Once an essential question has been identified and agreed upon by the learners, the next step might be to formulate a list of related questions that will assist the learner in answering the essential question. Often embedded within an essential question are subcategories that will generate questions that guide the learner's inquiry. For example, the essential question, "What makes a video game good?" might lead to subcategories such as graphics, ease of use, violence, and audience appropriateness, and may lead to subsequent questions, including "How do graphics affect the quality of the game?" or "How does ease of use contribute to its overall rating?"

Essential questions pass the "So what?" test. They are about matters of import.
            —Jamie McKenzie, *Learning to Question, to Wonder, to Learn*

Engaging Real-Life Scenarios

Engaging real-life scenarios help keep students focused on and excited about the big idea of the lesson, while integrating it with everyday life. Instead of asking a huge, overarching question, an engaging scenario sets the stage with a hypothetical, interesting, and very specific problem that students must solve. Engaging scenarios help students come back to the big idea and use all the knowledge they have learned. And here's a major bonus: the scenarios are built-in performance assessments.

At the start of the unit, you can have students write in their science journals about a prediction of how to solve the scenario question, and at the end of the unit, they can write about how they actually solved the question. Below are a number of engaging scenarios contributed by Stephanie Mikkelson, a teacher at Clayville Elementary in Clayville, Rhode Island, related to teaching water, balance, and motion concepts in science. These are from the teacher's point of view.

➡ I was doing laundry last night and I loaded the machine too high. When I did this, water sprayed up and splashed everywhere. I noticed that the water droplets looked different depending on what material it landed on. I asked myself, "What happens to water when it gets splashed or spilled on a surface?"

➡ After I looked at the different ways water interacts with different materials around my washing machine, I kept looking closely at the water droplets. The water continued to splash up after I added laundry detergent to the load of clothes. I noticed that the drops of water that contained plain water looked different from the drops of water that had

mixed with the soap. The drops with plain water looked like the drops of water we saw yesterday on the wax paper. Why does water make a dome on a flat surface? Why did the shape change when soap was added?

➡ As I hung out my clothes, it started to rain. In my rush to take the clothes off the line, I tipped over the plastic laundry basket. It lay sideways at a slight angle forming a slope. I noticed that different sized water droplets all moved in the same direction, but they did not travel at the same speed. What happens to the beads of water when they are dropped on a slope? How does the size of the drops affect their speed? The drops also changed speed when I put the laundry basket right side up again. How does the steepness of a slope affect the speed of water drops?

➡ I packed water for a picnic last weekend. I had filled the water up to the very top of the container because I wanted to have enough water for my family and I didn't want to pack another bottle. When I got to the picnic area, we played for a while before we ate. I forgot the container in the car and it got very hot inside. When I remembered the water, I noticed that the water had started to leak out of the top. My husband told me that since I was working on a water unit, I should have known that this would happen. As a scientist, what question should come to mind? ("What happens to water when it gets heated?") My husband told me not to open the water, but to put it in the cooler with lots of ice and the problem would be fixed. "Why?" I asked. "What happens to water when it gets cooled?"

➡ After the picnic, our friends invited us over to their house to go swimming. It was so nice outside, I couldn't wait to go in. I sat at the edge and put my toes in. It felt nice and warm. I jumped right in. To my surprise, the water at the bottom of the pool was cold! What do you think I asked myself? ("Why was the water warm at the top and cold at the bottom of the pool?")

➡ When I got home yesterday, I had to give my dog a bath. So I started running the hot water in the bathtub. By the time I got my dog upstairs into the bathroom, the water was getting cold. So I put more hot water in the tub. I noticed that this wasn't working too well, because the bath water was now warm on the top but the bottom was still cold. Why is that? What has happened?

➡ When I got home from the pool, I realized that we never drank the water in the bottle. By now, I knew that water when it gets colder takes up less space, so I figured I could throw it in the freezer. I was going to bring it to school the next day. Boy, was I surprised the next morning when I opened the freezer! ("What happens to water when it freezes?")

➡ All I had at home was a bag of crushed ice to stick in a container. I filled it to the top and looked forward to a big glass of cold water at lunch. When I took out the water from my school bag, I thought I had a leak because my container wasn't as full as it had been in the morning. My bag was dry. I asked myself, "What happened to the volume of water when the ice melted?" Now you know that water expands when it freezes. If you fill up water to the same height as the ice takes up in its container, which do you think would weigh more? What makes you say this?

Of course, it is possible to develop engaging scenarios for any subject area. A fractions lesson might start with a scenario about a pizza parlor, for example. Older students can develop engaging scenarios for one another. Not only will writing their own scenarios test your students' knowledge of the subject matter, but it will be a way to evaluate whether or not your students grasp the central tenets of the lesson.

One way to make sure you are engaging both boys and girls would be to let the students work in small single-gender groups and come up with scenario ideas. Are those ideas very different? Then use those ideas to develop scenarios in the content area you are teaching. Make sure that all students share in both scenarios created by boys and those created by girls.

Making It Matter: Culminating Projects

Culminating projects can help add authentic purpose to students' learning.

- Are your students learning right now about the effects of smoking?

    Have them write letters to high school students urging them not to start the habit.

- Are they learning about recycling?

    Start a recycling program at the school.

- Is your class right now studying the environment?

    Have the students write letters to the local newspaper about ways to reduce pollution.

Culminating projects raise students' performance and achievement. They can also be about finding ways to make a difference in the world.

The list of culminating projects that can really "make it matter" for kids is limited only by one's creativity. Here are a few ideas to get you started:

Letters   Have students write to the newspaper or elected official if they wish to express an opinion or persuade the public about an issue. Perhaps

it is a "Dear Abby" letter, a letter of complaint, or a letter to an author. Letter-writing can cut across all areas of the curriculum, including political issues (immigration, state testing), science (cloning, pollution), history (reminding the public about the significance of certain national holidays), education (the importance of education, homework policy), social issues (homelessness, civil rights), health education (exercise, nutrition), and more. Students can write to armed forces members stationed overseas, to local high schoolers about staying safe on prom night, to grandparents as part of a study about their ancestry or cultural traditions, or to a younger buddy in the school about an upcoming shared activity.

Public Service Announcements   Once students have identified an issue or topic, have them create a PSA directed at a character in a book or to the general public. Students can script and perform—and even film—their PSAs.

Interviews   Have students interview people who can add value to their studies. Cheri Merriman, a fifth-grade teacher, had her students interview war veterans. The students wove the veterans' recollections of the war into original historical fiction pieces. The veterans were then invited to attend a special reception in their honor at which each of the students read his or her piece and the individual veteran was introduced.

Student Newspaper   Get the kids some old blazers from Goodwill, make them an official-looking press badge, and have them select a school topic on which they can report. A digital camera is also a plus! A student newspaper doesn't need to be a regular publication. It's fine if it is done only one time as a culminating project for a specific unit of study. Consider publishing it on the Web to save paper and copying costs.

School Improvement Project   If your students are studying measurement or geometry, perhaps their skills can be put to use to advise the school on some playground improvements. Third grader Derek was allowed to take measurements and create a diagram of an ideal playground to demonstrate his learning about geometry and mapping skills. Other students honed their letter-writing skills by writing persuasive letters to the director of food services about the quality of the school's hot lunches. After studying about bullying prevention, a group of fifth graders developed informational posters to hang around the school and wrote and performed skits about how to deal with bullies for the other classes.

Documentary Projects   Allow students to use a digital still or movie camera and movie editing software to create simple "documentary films." Nowadays, with the aide of simple Web-based tutorials, older students can work mostly independently to acquire some basic movie editing skills that will help them create simple projects.

Social Action Projects   If your students feel strongly about a topic of study, maybe they can become part of the solution. Allow them to pursue opportunities to make a difference in the world in a real and meaningful way.

WISDOM OF PRACTICE FROM TEACHERS WHO MAKE IT MATTER

In her second-grade class, Sophie Trujillo-Schrock is teaching her students about New Orleans. The students are learning two jazz dances and will perform them along with their fourth-grade buddies at a performance for their parents. A clear sense of purpose is established for the second graders through both the collaboration and the performance outlet.

Mathematics instruction in Annie Keith's class takes place in a number of different settings. Every day first-grade and second-grade activities—such as sharing snacks, lunch count, and attendance—regularly serve as contexts for problem-solving tasks. Mathematics lessons make use of math centers in which the students do a variety of activities. On any given day, children at one center may solve word problems presented by the teacher while at another center children write word problems to present to the class later; at another, they play a math game.

Fifth graders Zach, Austin, and Eric are advanced students and often get their work done early. The school librarian has gotten them started on an iMovie project that they can work on as time allows. They've decided to create a narrated tour of the school telling visitors the most important things about the school.

Fourth-grade teacher Linda McCarthy and a group of fourth-grade students took concerns for the environment to heart. They began measuring the amount of waste generated each day in the school cafeteria and decided that they could reduce waste in the school by strengthening the school's recycling program and starting a composting program. Composting of food started in the cafeteria and now every classroom has a composting bucket. The group of fourth graders met regularly to discuss how the program was going and how to better educate the school community. They made announcements on the public address system, made and hung posters about reducing, recycling, and reusing, made presentations to classrooms, and visited recycling facilities.

Some elementary schools follow the MicroSociety model—a hands-on learning program that enables students to apply classroom skills in real-life ways. Three afternoons a week at Talbot Elementary School in Renton, Washington, students participate in a for-profit business, a government agency, or a nonprofit organization. For their businesses, students must create mission statements, business plans, and operating budgets. Students learn many financial and life lessons, as well as citizenship rights and responsibilities. Through running their businesses, students achieve a number of the Washington state content standards and express a high-degree of investment in their schoolwork.

Kindergarten teacher Jeanne Candler teaches her students about the life cycles of plants. Her students participate in the creation of a vegetable garden, including planting the seeds, watering, and weeding in the

(Continued)

spring. In the fall, the next group of kindergartners gets to harvest the crop and then, in the spring, start the cycle over again by planting a garden for the next group of kindergartners to harvest.

Gifted Education Advisor, Jill Maxwell, coordinates with fifth grade teachers to select fifteen students who are advanced in the areas of math and science. These students study flight with a community mentor. After presenting individual projects related to flight concepts, the students go to a regional airport and get to ride in a plane through the "Young Eagles" flight program, which is staffed by volunteer private pilots.

To wrap up a social studies unit related to the local community, second-grade teacher Laura Rickert takes her students to important historical locations in their neighboring town. Instead of going by school bus, Laura and her students research the city bus schedule, routes, and fares to plan a field trip around the community done entirely via public transportation.

Nancy Chiu's second graders study Alaska each year. A few years ago, she created a special version of the Iditarod for her students. Nancy calls it the I-kid-arod and the students have an Iditarod-themed field day with different races and activities—all based on different elements of the real race. One station hosts a sled-pulling race with a team of students pulling a student on a sled. At another station, students race to put on booties similar to what the sled dogs wear and then run a course. Students build igloo structures at another station with large blocks.

Notice how many of the activities in the box have components that would appeal up and down the brain gender spectrum!

"I'm going to be a football player so I should probably learn how to write a Bronco sign."

—Conor, second grader

WRAPPING UP THE MAIN POINTS

- Students care most about learning when it can be connected to real life and real purposes.

- There is often a disconnect between students' strengths and interests and what is taught in school.

- Generally, girls are more willing to do things simply to please their teacher. This may be due to socialization and can also be due to higher levels of certain neurotransmitters in the female brain.

- Teachers need to purposefully respect and involve students as central partners in learning.

- We can find out about students' interests, motivations, passions, and talents. We help our kids achieve more, perform better, and be better disciplined when we speak to their deep and hidden sense of personal purpose and relevance.

- A number of practical ways to create greater engagement by students are project-based learning, social action projects, healthy competition, simulation activities, and culminating projects.

Art Smart

7

Blending Art and Music into the Core Curriculum

Give me a laundry list and I'll set it to music.
　　　　　　　　　　　　　　—Gioacchionio Antonio-Rossini

WE are at a challenging time in education. The pressure to get high test scores seems to be a constant weight on the shoulders of educators. With a relatively short amount of time to net significant results, teachers and principals can feel pressured to find a magic bullet or a quick fix to get the rapid turnaround in scores that they need. Under this tremendous pressure to improve reading and math scores, many school districts have resorted to eliminating or greatly curtailing arts programs in favor of devoting more instructional time to the core curriculum.

Despite all of the current research on effective brain-based teaching, the "No Child Left Behind" education law has leveraged one of the most abrupt instructional shifts in the history of the United States. "Because of its emphasis on testing and accountability in particular subjects, it apparently forces some school districts down narrow intellectual paths," says Dr. William Reese, author of *America's Public Schools: From the Common School to No Child Left Behind.* "If a subject is not tested, why teach it?"

A recent survey by the Center on Education Policy found that since the passage of the federal law, 71 percent of the nation's fifteen thousand school districts had reduced the hours of instructional time spent on history, music, and other subjects to open up more time for reading and math. "Narrowing the curriculum has clearly become a nationwide pattern," said Jack Jennings, the president of the center, which is based in Washington.

When we as teachers succumb to this pressure, we lose track of the amazing "brain benefits" and learning assets that music, performance art, and visual art can provide. We also neglect the fact that students will do better on tests when they learn better throughout the year. Research over the last decade has elicited both qualitative and quantitative data to support the gains in test scores, grades, and classroom discipline through the careful and creative use of the arts in core curriculum.

A different, yet related, observation should give us pause: across the United States, community symphonies and arts organizations struggle, sometimes for their very existence. Could one reason be that we are not educating a new generation of young people to appreciate and thus support the arts in their communities? Civilization has long used the artistic gifts of prior generations to determine just how "civilized" they were. There may be many, many important reasons to make sure we are not ignoring arts education.

Why the Arts Work

Eric Jensen, author of *Arts with the Brain in Mind,* asserts, "The arts enhance the process of learning. The systems they nourish, which include our integrated sensory, attentional, cognitive, emotional and motor capacities are, in fact, the driving forces behind all other learning." Jensen contends that the arts serve as a developer of the brain. The arts provide learners with opportunities to develop and mature brain systems. Children's abilities to read, count, speak, and problem-solve are all correlated to the maturation of the brain. Researchers agree that aesthetic awareness, cultural exposure, social harmony, creativity, improved emotional expression, and appreciation of diversity are all supported by arts in school.

Specifically, there are key developmental periods during which exposure to music and music-making are critical. From birth through two years, the neurons in the auditory cortex are highly plastic and adaptive. Young children's brains are creating new neural networks all the time and need exposure to a variety of sounds. Ideally, children would start music lessons between the ages of three and eight, when left and right brain connectivity can be significantly enhanced.

Current research into the development of the adolescent brain has also shown that early adolescence, which begins in late elementary school for many children, is an optimal time for children to study music. Brain growth during this period offers exciting opportunities for learning. Studies show that children who start music lessons before or during early puberty show an increased lifelong potential for maintaining those skills, even when they stop and start again later in life. A direct link has been shown between literacy performance and music lessons!

Maturation of cortical areas linked to reading, counting, speaking, and problem solving is enhanced through performance opportunities. Specifically, involvement in the *performing arts* stimulates the vestibular system through movement and helps children think creatively, gain mastery, change points of view, and practice social skills.

In the area of the *visual arts*, research has found that a highly cognitive process involving problem solving, critical thinking, and creative thinking gains from drawing and other graphic development. Simple drawing forces us to visualize and plan our actions. Learning disability research has highlighted the use of visual arts; a recent study showed that drawing figures helped improve thinking skills and verbal skills in children with learning disabilities.

Boys and Girls and the Arts

Research on single-gender classes or grouping for art and music tends to show that boys will participate more fully in artistic endeavors when they aren't competing with girls. Girls tend to sing in tune better than boys (as much as seven times more often) and as they enter puberty (often in late elementary school) boys can be especially sensitive to this fact. They also are more aware of stereotypical expectations and are trying to be more "macho," not doing things girls do—such as dancing.

Adding artistic movement to single-gender physical education classes can help boys still enjoy being creative with movement and music without feeling the pressure they often perceive in coed groups. Pointing out that professional sports teams, including NFL football teams, often use dance to help improve balance and coordination in their players, can help some boys feel more comfortable. Also showing them videos of acclaimed male artists can be helpful. This is especially helpful in addressing self-esteem issues of boys who might fall into the stereotypical male role during this period of early adolescence.

In previous chapters, we have discussed the benefits of movement, visual-spatial strategies, social interaction, motivation and engagement. The arts can tie all of these strategies together to provide a number of benefits for both boys and girls. Let's draw it all together for a moment.

Movement

Activities such as dance can help in the formation of critical brain areas responsible for controlling spatial, visual, auditory, and motor functions. Even the simplest theater games and dance moves can energize and strengthen early brain function. Point out to your boys that early cultures, such as the Greeks, found men acting in all kinds of plays and doing all sorts of dances. Talk about Native American cultures in which both men and women learned traditional dances that told the stories of their people and their society, passing them on from one generation to the next.

Contact a local Native American cultural organization and have them visit your class or school, showing the boys and girls examples of how all members of the tribe participated in dance, music-making, and song.

Social Skills

Performing arts training is a powerful tool for developing the parts of the brain system involved in social functioning. The performing arts offer a high degree of social interaction, providing students with practice in reading facial expressions and body language, as well as encouraging self-expression and self-confidence. Music can assist children in identifying and regulating emotional states to enhance social functioning.

Emotional Intelligence

Performing arts give students the opportunity to release worries, tensions, and stress. Students learn to express a range of emotions. The visual arts can also help children express feelings without words. Working with clay can be a great way for both boys and girls to physically release tension—pounding clay is acceptable when pounding the desk, or each other, is not! Music helps students to experience and identify different emotions based on the mood of the music. Both the visual and the performing arts can be very therapeutic for these reasons.

Motivation

Students lacking motivation are harder to engage in classroom activities, and this can negatively affect their classroom performance and academic achievement. The performing arts can help these students find an area of passion and feel empowered. Through the arts, they are involved in making choices, moving their bodies, interacting socially, and performing for an audience. All of these mechanisms can turn a reluctant learner into an eager one. In addition, there are some students who struggle in every academic aspect of school but experience great success in the arts. And the more you can involve boys in arts programs in elementary school, the more likely they will be to continue that involvement in middle school, smoothing the transition to secondary. Participation in the arts decreases the chance that a student will drop out by 15 percent.

Self-Discipline

The visual and performing arts often require great persistence, teamwork, focus, and determination. Girls' relationship imperatives encourage their involvement in these kinds of activities. Boys' task focus and goal orientation can be called into play with similar results. Students must engage their attentional systems along with their cognitive, perceptual-motor, memory, and visual, and auditory systems. Practicing and rehearsing require a huge amount of effort that can enhance all of these cognitive abilities, as well as students' self-discipline.

Cognition

A number of studies have demonstrated a relationship between participation in the arts and academic achievement. A longitudinal Japanese study showed that both boys and girls involved in music lessons performed better in literacy testing—and that this performance improvement continuing to show up a year after music lessons ended. Further, students who are involved in the arts increasingly look forward to coming to school. Student engagement, motivation, problem solving, creativity, and improved relationships can all lead to better academic results.

Memory

Memory systems are activated through improved listening, attention, concentration, and recall. When children respond to music, a series of neurotransmitters are released in the brain, and when that music is connected to a positive emotional experience, it triggers positive responses far into the future, sometimes throughout life. Emotional experiences caused by or associated with music result in more detailed recall of events. Some studies have shown that when music is played during periods of learning and then played during testing on that same learning, recall tends to increase.

The arts are fundamental resources through which the world is viewed, meaning is created, and the mind developed.

—Elliot W. Eisner

We need less trivia and more in-depth learning about the things that matter the most in our world: order, integrity, thinking skills, a sense of wonder, truth, flexibility, fairness, dignity, contribution, justice, creativity, and cooperation. Does that sound like a tall order? The arts can do all that.

—Eric Jensen

Focusing on the Musical Arts

Musical arts include listening, playing, singing, composing, arranging, and reading music. Cave painting depicting the use of music goes back seventy thousand years. Thirty-thousand-year-old flutes have been found in France. Animals and early humans used music to communicate with one another to warn of danger and enhance social bonding. Music has helped us learn for millennia and still can continue to do so.

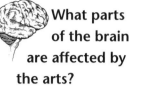

What parts of the brain are affected by the arts?

Left temporal lobes: a key "math area" of the brain that is also highly involved with music. Studies show a correlation between music-making and increased spatial awareness and problem solving.

Nucleus basalis: located in the midbrain, this area gives weighted emotional meaning to auditory input. Studies suggest that music improves emotional awareness.

Primary auditory area: area of the brain responsible for hearing reception. Increased thickness of layer four of the auditory cortex has been discovered in the brains of accomplished musicians.

Reticular activating system: the center of balance for the other systems involved in learning, self-control or inhibition, and motivation. It provides the neural connections that are needed for the processing and learning of information, and the ability to pay attention to the correct task.

Occipital lobes: this area of the brain is used for visual input and visualizing. Specifically, it is responsible for color recognition and controls vision.

Parietal lobes: this part of the brain is responsible for sensory sorting, spatial orientation, and visual perception.

Student Comments

"Music helps a lot because it usually calms my mind and makes me think of more creative ideas."

—5th grade girl

"Having music played in a classroom is very helpful because it can put you in a mood for writing something."

—5th grade boy

"Music helps me if it's a song with no lyrics or if I don't know the song. Otherwise, I would sing along and get off topic."

—5th grade girl

"Music is good for me. It calms me and its good for my mind by making my body feel better."

—5th grade girl

Songs That Promote Learning

There are a number of professionally produced songs available that tie to every content area and skill imaginable. A quick search on the Web will yield many results. Additionally, simple children's song lyrics can be changed to incorporate the skills being taught. For older children, it's fun to have them do a "Children's Song Remake." Have them select a favorite children's song and modify the lyrics to incorporate the concepts that have been learned. Let them work as a group to practice their teamwork skills and give them an opportunity to perform in front of the class. Consider purchasing a karaoke (no vocals) CD so the students' performances can have back-up music. They'll have a blast!

To get you started, here is a list of children's songs:

Boom, Boom, Ain't It Great to Be Crazy

The Wheels on the Bus

The Farmer in the Dell

Three Blind Mice

Twinkle, Twinkle Little Star

She'll Be Comin' Around the Mountain

Five Green and Speckled Frogs

I've Been Working on the Railroad

Miss Mary Mack

The Itsy-Bitsy Spider

There Were Ten in the Bed

Yankee Doodle

Row Row Row Your Boat

Happy Birthday

Ring Around the Rosey

London Bridge

This Old Man

Mary Had a Little Lamb

———————

Here are a number of children's songs that have already been "re-made" to teach phonics. These lyrics are written by Debra Renner Smith at www.debfourblocks.com:

1. (tune: "If You're Happy and You Know It")
If you think you know this word raise your hand (2x)
If you think you know this word that you just heard,
If you think you know this word raise your hand.
(supply a word, stretching it out; for example, c-a-t)

2. (tune: "Twinkle, Twinkle Little Star")
Listen, listen to my word
Tell me all the sounds you heard: /Cat/ (say this slowly and wait a moment)
/c/ is one sound, /a/ is two
/t/ is last in /cat/ it's true!
(at the end sing):
Thanks for listening to my words
and telling me the sounds you heard!

3. (tune: "Jimmy Cracked Corn and I Don't Care")
Who has a /d/ word to share with us?
Who has a /d/ word to share with us?
Who has a /d/ word to share with us?
It must start with the /d/ sound!
(call on children to supply word and class sings this together)
Dog is a word that starts with /d/
Dog is a word that starts with /d/
Dog is a word that starts with /d/
Dog starts with the /d/ sound.

4. (tune: "Old MacDonald Had a Farm")
What's the sound that starts these words:
Turtle, time, and teeth?
(wait for a response from the children)
/t/ is the sound that starts these words:
turtle, time, and teeth.
With a /t/, /t/ here, and a /t/, /t/ there,
Here a /t/, there a /t/, everywhere a /t/, /t/.
/t/ is the sound that starts these words:
Turtle, time, and teeth!
You all did great, now clap your hands!
(clap, clap, clap, clap, clap)
(you can use beginning sounds, medial sounds, or final sounds)

5. (tune: "Skip to my Lou")
Silly Willy, who should I choose? (repeat 3x)
I choose. _____ (Terry, berry)
(continue the song using students' names)

6. (tune: "Have You Ever Seen a Lassie")

Did you ever see a cat, a cat, a cat,

Did you ever see a cat sit on a rat?

r-at, c-at

r-at, c-at,

Did you ever see a cat sit on a rat?

(repeat the verse using other animal rhyming words)

7. (tune: "If You're Happy and You Know It")

If your name begins with /m/, stand up,

If your name begins with /m/, stand up,

If your name begins with /m/, stand up and take a bow,

If your name begins with /m/, stand up.

(you can also use this with pictures; "If your picture begins with /s/, stand up")

8. (tune: "A Hunting We Will Go")

A searching we will go, a searching we will go,

We'll find an /h/ and add a /orse/,

And now we have a horse!

9. (chant)

It begins with /t/,

And it ends with /im/.

Put them together,

And they say _____. (Tim)

10. (tune: "The Wheels on the Bus")

The sounds in the word go /c/ /a/ /t/; /c/ /a/ /t/; /c/ /a/ /t/.

The sounds in the word go /c/ /a/ /t/,

Can you guess the word?

———————————

You can also find published original songs that help to reinforce concepts from all curricular areas in fun and engaging ways—typically, these incorporate corresponding hand and body movements. One fun example would be "The Vowel Family Song" by Cathy Bollinger from the *Alphabet Jam Album.*

Wisdom of Practice: Teachers Who Use the Musical Arts

Kindergarten teacher Sarah Shrum uses the tune "Chitty Chitty Bang Bang," from the Disney movie, to get her students moving. "I add statements and movements, like 'I can move my body' (move your whole body), 'I can do karate' (act out karate), 'I can move my hips' (move your hips) or 'I can close my lips' (finger in front of mouth 'shhhhhhhh')."

From K–3 teacher Candace Robison: "This is an activity that I learned as a drum major in high school, but it works even better for second graders! When students are getting antsy, or even better, after they have been working hard for a good stretch of time, this is a good way to help them get the wiggles out. Students need a good amount of space, for safety's sake. There's a certain rhythm to it, a bit like a poem, but it's more a chant than a song so you don't really need a melody."

> Hello! My name is Joe. I have a house, three kids, and one spouse. I work in a button factory. One day, my boss came up to me and he said, "Hey, Joe! Are you busy?" I said, "No." He said, "Push this button with your right elbow." (Students take pointer finger and imitate pushing a button, making sure that they push from the elbow.)

"You do the activity over again, each time using a new body part (left elbow, right knee bone, left knee bone, head bone). By the end of the song, their whole bodies are moving, and when the boss asks if Joe is busy, students yell, 'YES!' Students love it and it really gets their brains ready for another stretch of thinking."

Teacher Julie IntVeld shares: "There is a great song called 'Chicken Lips and Lizard Hips' on a CD titled 'For Our Children.' It's about a boy that doesn't like what mom makes for dinner so she makes something with chicken lips and lizard hips and alligator eyes . . . It's really easy to add movements to the song and keep the kids moving."

Music teacher Tula Roberge integrates the academic curriculum into music class on a regular basis. Fifth graders studying the Civil War learn to sing African spiritual songs. Second graders learn to sing songs and play instruments and games as part of their study of Australia. The school musical has been based on social studies themes, such as the Industrial Revolution and immigration.

For very young children, pre-K and kindergarten, Peter, Paul and Mary's rendition of "I'm Being Swallowed by a Boa Constrictor" really gets the kids moving, singing simple words, and giggling—always a positive activity! And it can be connected to a science lesson on snakes.

Katherine Lawson is a music specialist at Cedar Valley, a K–8 school in the Edmonds School District in Lynnwood, Washington, just north of Seattle. 89 percent of her school's students receive free lunches, and there are thirty-one different languages spoken at the school. All but a few of the kindergarteners receive ELL support services and the numbers stay fairly high at all grade levels. The schools' service area includes

Different Music at Different Times—Change the Music, Change the State

Music *before* class. As students file into class in the morning or after lunch, music can serve to mark the routines that children are to follow—hang up coats and backpacks, take lunch count, set up chairs, and meet in the circle area. If students are familiar with the song, they can be sure that they finish all their tasks by the time the song ends. Music that is tied to the curriculum can set the stage for the unit of study (such as music from different regions). Upbeat music can put students in a positive mood before they start their lessons.

Music *during* class. Music works well when students are in small discussion groups or working on a project. Background music can increase students' willingness to talk; since the room isn't silent, they aren't concerned about other groups overhearing. Sound from other groups also tends to be less disruptive when there is music in the background to "pad" the effect. In general, it is best to go with predictable music without words so that the music itself does not serve as a distraction. You might try traditional classical music, such as Bach's Brandenburg Concertos, Handel's Water Music, or Vivaldi's Four Seasons. You can also consider environmental sounds, such as waves, waterfall, or forest soundtracks.

Music works well during transitions as well. If you need students to clean up one activity and move to another, set it to music and challenge them to be ready by the time the song ends. The music will energize the kids to move with greater efficiency and focus, and they'll have enjoyed an energy boost as they start into the next activity.

Music *after* class. As students prepare to go to lunch or wrap up their day to go home, music can be played so that they will leave with a positive feeling and in a happy mood. Again, given that these are transition times, the music can be used to frame the time during which students need to complete all the required tasks. Some teachers like to sing a song as a class at the end of each school day or at the end of the week. This can provide a sense of unity and fun.

many low-income apartments and many of the students move sometime during the school. Less than 10 percent stay at Cedar Valley for more then five years. All classrooms have a few students who are autistic, ADD, or ADHD. Katherine shares:

> What works well for me is consistent rituals. Younger classes enter the room to find their specific seat location while singing an entrance song. I use the same one for kindergarten all year, and vary the leaving ritual song adding a second one mid-year. Older classes enter listening to the composer-of-the-month music. Info to aid in listening is on the board. Classes leave by taking turns being a conductor. There is a specific routine they follow to be the conductor.

Katherine is able to help her students, whose lives may offer limited structure and stability, by providing rituals in the learning environment, with music as the tool. This structure adds a sense of safety, making it easier for her students to learn. And because Katherine, as a music teacher, gets to work with children as they move up through the grades, she provides a consistent figure in their otherwise often changing lives. In this situation, music is truly a part of core curriculum.

Using Technology with Music

The advent of MP3 players makes it much easier for teachers to collect and organize their musical selections for the classroom—no more CDs to store, search through, and load. This setup requires the purchase of an MP3 player and an accompanying stereo system that docks the player. Songs can be downloaded from the Internet or from your current selection of CDs. Perhaps the most convenient aspect of using an MP3 player is that your song selections can be organized into "playlists." Playlists can be set up according to use (such as background music or brain breaks), by the subject area they relate to, or by musical style. Note: If you purchase an MP3 player with a built-in microphone, you can also make recordings of students' classroom performances, oral reports, and readings.

Students can now compose original scores on the computer. There are even keyboards that can be attached to the computer. With or without a keyboard, software programs such as Music Ace Deluxe allow students to drag-and-drop notes onto a staff and select the instruments to be played in their composition. Adding this "virtual space" arena to music class is great for the spatially oriented boys and good exercise for the more verbally oriented girls!

Focusing on the Visual Arts

The visual arts include a wide variety of activities, including drawing, painting, illustrating, photography, sculpture, costume design, makeup, lighting, props, scenery, filmmaking, printmaking, and computer-based graphics design. This is another opportunity to find amateur and professional artists in your community, both male and female, to visit your classroom or school to make presentations about their work. There have been famous artists of both genders throughout history, and often children are not familiar with them or their work. Learning about these role models can help children see the larger world of possibilities, and encourage boys or girls who may have an interest in the arts that hasn't been identified.

Historians tend to agree that art-making may have emerged as early as 1.5 million years ago with the arrival of *Homo erectus,* our human-like ancestors. They used iron oxide pigments for nonutilitarian tasks, showing a clear propensity for art-making behavior. Cave painting and early sketching were likely ways to enhance thinking, serving as a medium for idea manipulation, enhancement, and storage. Art served as a kind of visual sketchpad for thinking—and still does today.

Some evidence indicates that the benefits of the visual arts for children are greater when they are started earlier, suggesting a developmental role in the process. As children grow into adolescents, it is important to encourage them to continue to draw, organize, paint, design, and build. It is these same skills that are often identified as critical for many occupations, including dentists, surgeons, graphic artists, and tradespeople.

There are strong indicators that a big part of art is its ability to evoke an emotional response. Ramachandran and Hirstein suggest, "Humans are different from other species: We do art for the mere pleasure of it. Making and observing visual art seems to enhance our ability to elicit and even mediate our emotional responses."

Use of the visual arts via graphic organizers, drawing pictures and symbols, visualizing, and building physical models was addressed in detail in Chapter Three, "Make It Visual." If you are interested in expanding your repertoire of skills in the classroom with the visual arts, be sure to refer to that chapter.

My Little Beach Glass
By: McCall

Have you ever seen glass being formed by the waves? Well, if
you have, have you ever seen one that is colored like a romantic
African sunset in the Masi Mara?
Feel it. It is as bumpy as stairs leading to a basement. It is as hard
as a shiny piece of metal. It is the same size as a new
quarter. Look at it. It is as shiny as a new face of a watch.
Pick it up. It is as light as a small skipping stone.
As you can see, it makes a difference when it gets formed by the
waves.

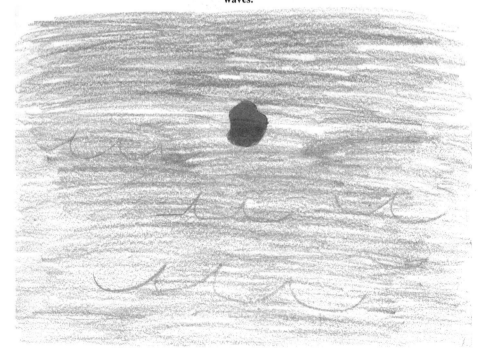

This second grader's piece was written after time spent visualizing and drawing. Note the extent of the sensory detail that this student was able to include in her piece. This is a simple yet powerful example of integrating the visual arts in the classroom curriculum.

Wisdom of Practice: Teaching Using the Visual Arts

Art teacher Diane Deyo incorporates the classroom curriculum into her art instruction. First graders studying Japan do ink drawings of bamboo in the traditional Japanese style. Fifth graders create watercolor paintings of the rainforest animals. Second graders craft didgeridoos to complement their study of Australia.

Second-grade teacher Mary Jo Barbeau has students write poetry and create watercolor pictures of the aurora borealis as part of their study of Alaska.

Computer assistant Dawne Mangus turns off all of the lights in the computer lab. Students close their eyes as she leads them through a visualization and listening exercise. When they open their eyes, they use KidPix to illustrate four powerful images that they saw in their mind's eye.

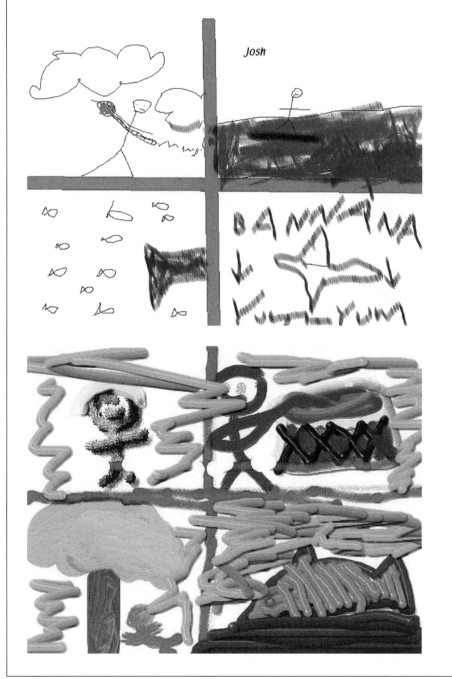

Josh

Fifth graders in Leann Mullineaux's class create narrative non-fiction pieces about the rainforest. They illustrate the books extensively with beautiful pastel drawings.

Using Technology with the Visual Arts

Technology can be motivational for all children, especially those who may be reluctant to engage in drawing or painting in the more traditional ways. You may decide to use technology for all of your students on some occasions and for select students at other times. For students who complete the assignment early or need a more challenging culminating project, technology can serve as an excellent resource and tool. It can also be a great motivator.

The strong smell of urine drifts through the air and daintily slides in to my nostrils. My nose shoots up in the air and sniffs. Sure enough, the urine smell belongs to a devious male, and it is coming from my leaf den. I jump to my feet and anxiously bound away towards my leaf den.

After about three minutes of running, a small clearing with a quiet river surrounded by palm trees comes into view. The strong smell of urine swells and swirls in my nostrils. I run as fast as my legs will allow to the den. I finally come to the edge of a pitiful pile of leaves that I think might be where the smell is coming from. I bend my head and smell the leaves. A missile of strong smelling urine explodes in my nostrils. The smell is definitely coming from here. I bend my head once again and inhale the essence of the smell from the leaves. The smell flies through my nostrils and my head and rests in my brain. My brain then analyzes this smell. After careful investigation, my brain concludes this: A male, recently matured, who didn't have a territory, has marked his territory on my leaf den, therefore challenging me. It also tells me I should be aware.

Graphic Organizers

Created for K–5 learners, Kidspiration is a software program that provides an easy way to apply the proven principles of visual learning. Students build graphic organizers by combining pictures, text, and spoken words to represent thoughts and information. Younger learners develop early literacy skills, and more advanced students improve comprehension skills and better organize ideas for writing. Support for emerging technologies offers more options for applying Kidspiration in your classroom. Use Kidspiration with interactive whiteboards to encourage whole-class collaboration in brainstorming, organization, and writing activities.

Drawing and Painting on the Computer

Two good programs to allow students to draw and paint with technology are KidPix and Adobe Photoshop. Without getting too technical, you can create graphics on a computer in two ways:

- *Drawing* in a software application means using tools that create "objects," such as squares, circles, lines, or text, which the program treats as discrete units. If you draw a square in Photoshop, for example, you can click anywhere on the square and move it around or resize it. It's an object, just like typing the letter *e* in a word processor.

- *Painting* in an application, in contrast, doesn't create objects. If you look at a computer screen, you'll see that it's made up of millions of tiny dots called pixels. You'll see the same thing in a simpler form if you look at the color comics in the Sunday newspaper—lots of dots (in four colors of ink) that form a picture. Unlike a drawing function, a painting function changes the color of individual pixels based on the tools you choose. In a photograph of a person's face, for example, the colors change gradually because of light, shadow, and complexion. You need a paint function to create this kind of effect.

Multimedia Tools

Two good choices for creating multimedia presentations with kids are HyperStudio and PowerPoint. Both applications allow students to present their knowledge in a slide-show format that is fairly simple and straightforward to use. Additionally, PowerPoint has many features for advanced users and would provide a wonderful challenge (including the use of customized animation of graphics and effects) for your students who need additional challenge.

Digital Stills and Movies

Perhaps you've decided to have students do a documentary for their culminating project. Students can use digital technology to take still photos or movie footage. A photo editing program such as Adobe Photoshop will give students experience with an application that most professionals use. For digital movies, students can use an editing application such as iMovie or Toast.

Focusing on the Performing Arts

The performing arts encompass dance, drama, directing, choreography, kinesthetic awareness, improvisation, plays, mime, musicals, and other media play. Children who pursue the performing arts rarely continue as professionals in the field. The real driving force behind getting children engaged in the dramatic arts are the benefits for children emotionally, physically, and cognitively.

The performing arts naturally integrate across the curriculum. An excellent resource for ideas on using the performing arts to enhance reading comprehension can be found in Jeffrey Wilhelm's *Action Strategies for Deepening Reading Comprehension.* Wilhelm advocates for the use of "enactments"—inviting students to imagine together, actively depicting characters, forces, or ideas, and to interact in the roles. These enactments are not unlike role-plays. As are the performing arts, enactments are action-oriented and participatory. Enactments

- Require students to work together, express their opinions, listen to each other, and create meaning together

- Require active involvement by all parties

- Provide a variety of roles and ways to participate

- Begin with and are driven by student interests, by what they already know and find significant and by what is socially relevant

- Develop new interests in students

The arts must be at the heart of every child's learning experience if . . . they are to have a chance to dream and to create, to have beliefs, to carry a sense of cultural identity.
    —James D. Wolfensohn, former chairman of the Kennedy Center

Practical Ideas for Your Classroom

In addition to these activity ideas, be sure to check out the Practical Ideas section in Chapter Two. A number of the brain break ideas incorporate music. These activities are great for both boys and girls!

➡ Keep a box of wooden sticks and blocks, maracas, and other rhythm instruments in your classroom for keeping the beat in a fun way.
➡ Provide quality background music, such as Mozart's Sonata for Two Pianos in D Major or Haydn's Symphonies no. 42, 45, 56, 94, and 100, and works by Gershwin or Oscar Peterson.

➡ Have students dance or move to one song as a transition between lessons or activities. Remind students they need to be at their expect spots by the end of the song. This works best when using the same song or songs so that students are familiar with the length of the song.

➡ Have students sit in their chairs. Play upbeat music and have them dance while sitting—the sillier the better.

➡ Greet your students in the morning with the song "In the Mood" by Glenn Miller.

➡ Alert the class that it's lunch time with "Be Our Guest" from *Beauty and the Beast*.

➡ At the end of the school day, send your students off with "So Long, Farewell" from *The Sound of Music.*

➡ With calming music playing in the background, have students close their eyes. Have them take a few deep cleansing breaths and then provide a concise review of the learning material.

➡ Have students collect a number of visual art examples, including CD covers, marketing materials, or t-shirts. Have them analyze the use of color, contrast, and motion. How does the artist use art to communicate a message?

➡ Use technology tools to create visual arts. Students who don't think that they can draw paint or design may develop new skills with the help of technology.

➡ Get students involved with building and designing sets for a classroom or school play. Have them figure the costs of supplies, measure and cut the materials, and construct the set. This is a great way to integrate math and science skills.

➡ Learn the music and dances of the part of the world that you are studying. Dance to the music frequently throughout the day.

➡ Write a grant to purchase an MP3 player and a sound system. Build playlists that correspond to the different content areas and uses of music (such as energizing or calming).

WRAPPING UP THE MAIN POINTS

- Because of high-stakes testing and NCLB, school districts are facing mounting pressure to improve reading and math scores. As a result, some schools and districts have cut arts programs, especially for low-performing students, without realizing that these cuts can ultimately lead to more student failure, not less.

- There is a correlation between the arts and academic performance, motivation, self-esteem, and social skills. Arts develop the human brain and an early start appears to increase the benefits.

- Music can be used strategically before, during, and after instruction. Consideration must be given to what kinds of music and how much music is used to maximize the benefits to students. Students can participate in listening to, singing, and composing music. Learning songs can help reinforce academic concepts.

- Performing arts can help students in many areas, especially in language arts.

- The visual arts—even just simple drawing—enhances students' thinking, planning, and verbal skills.

- There are excellent technology applications available to enhance the integration of the arts.

Music expresses that which cannot be said and on which it is impossible to be silent.

—Victor Hugo

All children are artists. The problem is how to remain an artist once he grows up.

—Pablo Picasso

Connecting with Your Students

8

Promoting Learning Through Teacher-Child Relationships

Everything starts with relationship. Connect with them, get on their level, find out their interests.

—Bill Smith, third-grade teacher

ALL of us can probably remember a teacher who deeply affected our lives. We probably had at least one of these in elementary school. We may have decided to go into education in part because of these teachers. We know the hunger in a young learner for the teacher of significance, the teacher who admires the student's individual gifts, the teacher who connects with the heads and the hearts of students.

In his book *Teacher and Child,* Haim Ginott, an oft-cited psychologist and educator, wrote

> I've come to the frightening conclusion that I am the decisive element in the classroom. It's my personal approach that creates the climate. It's my daily mood that makes the weather. As a teacher, I possess a tremendous power to make a person's life miserable or joyous. I can be a tool of torture or an instrument of inspiration. I can humiliate or humor, hurt or heal. In all situations, it is my response that decides whether a crisis will be escalated or de-escalated or a person humanized or de-humanized.

Teachers have long recognized the importance of developing caring relationships with their students. Connecting with young people is often the most powerful motivator of learning for students. A strong teacher-student relationship can go a long way towards raising children's self-esteem, creating a caring learning environment, and promoting academic growth. In fact, one of the best predictors of students' effort and engagement in school is the relationships they have with their teachers. Some very practical thinking and strategies can help you connect and reconnect with your boys and girls.

Why Personal Connections with Students Work

The most effective teachers subscribe to the belief that before they attempt to teach a student academic skills or content, they must first create a safe and secure environment. We are all familiar with the adage, "They don't care what you know until they know that you care." The relationships between children and teachers, though not the same as parent-child relationships, are often most successful when they employ the same kind of sensitive, responsive interactions that are the hallmarks of a healthy attachment between parents and children.

One of the foremost researchers in the area of motivation is psychologist Edward Deci at the University of Rochester. Deci's research shows that students will be more motivated to learn when the following needs have been met: to feel a sense of belonging and connectedness to the school; to feel a sense of autonomy and self-determination; and to feel competent.

He argues that developing a positive, supportive relationship with students is the key to building a classroom environment that meets these needs.

Echoing Deci's findings, researchers have consistently shown that positive teacher-student relationships, defined as warm, close, and communicative, are linked to behavioral competence and better school adjustment. Troubles in teacher-student relationships are also related to a negative school attitude, school avoidance, and hostile aggression. The teacher's care and affection matters!

And it matters even more when there is too little emotional connection to a caregiver at home. Supportive school experiences play a critical role in students' adaptations to school. Emotionally supportive teachers are one of the factors that decrease the vulnerability of high-risk students to stressful life events.

A study completed by the Massachusetts Department of Education detailed the significant role of educators: "Possibly the most critical element to success within school is a student developing a close and nurturing relationship with at least one caring adult. Students need to feel that there is someone whom they know, to whom they can turn, and who will act as an advocate for them."

Does High-Stakes Testing Have to Get in the Way of Teacher-Student Connections?

Psychologist Richard Ryan and others have found that high-stakes tests tend to constrain teachers' choices about curriculum coverage and curtail their ability to respond to students' interests. Also, psychologists Tim Urdan and Scott Paris have found that such tests can decrease teacher enthusiasm for teaching, which has an adverse effect on teacher-student relationships and, thus, on students' motivation.

"I've been teaching more years than I'd like to admit and it seems to me students have shortened attention spans today and often many struggle to focus and remember. . . . I'm afraid the flashing video games, poor nutrition, lack of adult attention at home, and lack of proper sleep is robbing our children of being able to truly learn. Families that move their children from school to school year after year are doing a disservice to their children. They need a place of community and caring where they can make friends and bond with a teacher. Even when a child finds learning difficult it's easier to persevere when the teacher knows you and can cheer you on. The student can also focus more when they trust the teacher who encourages their efforts."

—Katherine Larson, elementary music teacher

Yet, the empirical evidence remains: the teacher-student relationship has been identified as a significant influence on overall academic and behavioral success. How do we juggle? This chapter will provide you with a number of very effective tools for building connectivity no matter the pressure you are under.

? **DID YOU KNOW? The Role of the Teacher-Student Connection Is Valued All Over the World**

In the Christian tradition, Jesus was called "the teacher," and he taught through close relationships with disciples. The Christian religion has taken the concept of connectivity with the teacher to its most detailed outcome—in order for anyone to fully understand God's important precepts, they must commit their heart (their emotional core) to the teacher, Jesus.

Farther east, in the tradition of Chi Gung and T'ai Chi, the student-teacher relationship is based on mutual trust, respect, and honor. The student makes a commitment, first to him- or herself to improve the quality of health and life, and second to the teacher, giving the teacher respect, open and honest communication, and loyalty. The teacher is the vehicle to the teachings, and can help develop a deep connection and understanding of the teachings.

In similar Buddhist teachings, the daily experience is a life path, and connections with students and others are one of the best vehicles for growing on that path. Buddhists believe that in order for the path to unfold, relationships must become conscious, not merely implied or suggested. Being conscious of the student-teacher relationship of caring, compassion, and love helps teachers and students develop greater awareness, depth, and spirit.

In the Muslim tradition, especially the Sufi tradition, the most important moral, social, and economic information is best imparted through the teacher-student connection. Mohammed is the teacher of peace. Students learn in individual and group *medrese* (classrooms) how to achieve peace.

In the Jewish Kabbalah, the relationship between student and teacher, if it is to be maximally productive, must reflect certain attitudes and commitments of each to the other. The teacher has three levels of responsibility to his students. The first is fulfillment of the prerequisite of getting to know students individually. Second, the teacher must express love and affection toward the students. It is this affection that dissolves the students' natural tendency to resist being told what to do. Finally, the teacher must take time to reflect upon his students' progress, refining and adjusting his vision of how best to influence them toward positive change.

Current teaching environments—though taking place in a modern democracy and separating church from state—are actually new forms of very old traditions. Not surprisingly, there is no ethnic or tribal group in the past that did not value teacher-students relationship as being nearly on a par with parental relationships. Our ancestors have always given our civilization's highest aspirations, principles, and cultural information to our teachers.

What Experts Have Said

"A fundamental question for a student is 'Does my teacher like me?' Given a rigorous, aligned curriculum, the answer to that simple question is our best predictor of student achievement."

—*Alice Terry,* More Life Through Management

"The quality of teacher–student relationships is the keystone for all other aspects of classroom management."

—*Marzano and Marzano,* Dimensions of Learning

"We cannot teach students well if we do not know them well."

—*Theodore Sizer*

"A strong relationship with a caring adult enables at-risk youth to make life-altering changes."

—*Werner and Smith,* Overcoming the Odds: High Risk Children from Birth to Adulthood

"80 percent of students entering schools feel good about themselves. By the end of fifth grade only 20 percent do. Only one in five high school students have positive self-esteem.

—*National Assessment of Educational Progress,* National Parent Teacher Association, 1990

A word as to the education of the heart: We don't believe that this can be imparted through books; it can only be imparted through the loving touch of the teacher.

—Cesar Chavez

The Head and the Heart: How the Brain Influences the Student-Teacher Bond

Oxytocin: helps us trust other people. When trust is established, oxytocin can rise, making the student more resistant to stress and social phobias. Females have more oxytocin than males and the receptors are found in the nucleus accumbens of the brain. They will tend to minimally trust a teacher more quickly than a male will.

Vasopressin: considered to be the "male equivalent" of the receptor oxytocin. It is found in the ventral pallidum and is linked to social bonding, especially in males. It is a factor in what you may have seen in class or in the halls: males often like to bond through contests or hierarchical jesting. Teachers can often exploit this proclivity and build better bonds with males.

Dopamine: the dopamine system of the nucleus accumbens produces the rewarding and sometimes addictive effects of sex, food, and drugs of abuse. Neuroscientists believe that the same reward pathways are likely stimulated during and following pair-bond formation.

Limbic System: comprised of a number of connected structures involved in emotional response, including the hypothalamus, amygdala, thalamus, fornix, hippocampus, and cingulate gyrus.

One looks back with appreciation to the brilliant teachers, but with gratitude to those who touched our human feelings. The curriculum is so much necessary raw material, but warmth is the vital element for the growing plant and for the soul of the child.

—Carl Jung

Being the Charismatic Adult

Dr. Robert Brooks, a noted clinical psychologist, lectures extensively on the topic of developing resiliency in children. He identifies one of the key protective factors for children as the presence of a "charismatic adult"—an adult with whom they can identify and from whom they can gather strength. And in a surprising number of cases, that person turns out to be a teacher.

How does one become a charismatic adult in a student's life? Dr. Brooks asked educators to recall their most positive memories of their own schooling. Often, it is the seemingly small gestures that have the most enduring impact. A charismatic teacher offers a smile, a warm greeting, a note of encouragement, a few minutes to meet alone with a student when indicated, and an appreciation and respect for different learning styles. These gestures are powerful demonstrations of acceptance and caring.

Forming meaningful connections with students also benefits the teacher. Becoming a charismatic adult in the life of a student can enhance the sense of meaning that teachers experience in their work, thereby lessening feelings of disillusionment and burnout. This, in turn, can decrease stress and allow teachers to be more open and accepting toward their students. For more information about developing resiliency and the role of charismatic adults, read Dr. Brooks's writings at www.drrobertbrooks.com.

A Self-Reflection Activity

Using the postcard shown below, write a message to the person who gave you your first memory of school. To whom would you write? Do you remember the person's name? Was it a good memory? Did that person have an influence on how you felt about school or your decision to become a teacher? Why? Is it possible for you to actually send a postcard to that person today?

To: The Person Who
Gave Me My First
Memory of School

Use this activity as a model for challenging yourself to write at least two postcards to the parents of each child in your class during the school year. Have the school office print two sets of labels addressed "To the parents of . . ." each of your students. Put the labels on the postcards and keep them in a file so you will know who still needs a postcard as the weeks go by.

In each postcard, share something positive about the child. Ask the parents to share the postcard with their child, perhaps over dinner. For some children, this may be the first (or the only) time their parents have received a positive message from a teacher! Teachers using this activity have had wonderful responses from both children and parents.

Student Comments

"I know that adults care for me when they show me they're really interested in my work and they help to make it better."

—5th grade boy

"If teachers didn't care about me, they wouldn't care about my knowledge. So if they didn't care, I wouldn't be here."

—5th grade boy

"Mrs. King knows every student's name. When she recognizes your work, you feel good and you know people care."

—3rd grade boy

"Usually, when I do something good or do my best on something, the adults recognize it and compliment my work. They also help me improve myself everyday. If they weren't interested in me, they wouldn't do these things."

—3rd grade girl

"The teachers show a lot of interest in our writing. They really care about how we want it and help us revise it to our liking."

—3rd grade girl

Capturing Kids' Hearts

Rigor, Relevance and Relationships are at the heart of an educational program called "Capturing Kids' Hearts." These "three Rs" are so important that teachers in participating schools and districts receive extensive training that is designed to build productive relationships between teachers and students. The program is based on the philosophy of program founder M. B. Flippen, "If you have a child's heart, you have his head."

Denver Public Schools Executive Director David Sneed reports, "Through this approach teachers treat students with more respect and students take more ownership for their behavior. Kids monitor themselves and their peers, while teachers are able to do the teaching and coaching that they need to do in the classroom. We feel confident that the end result will be improved schools and more student learning."

The participating Denver schools have reduced class transitions, improved orientation for new students, and made additional structural changes to reduce disruptions. Greeting students at the classroom door, shaking hands with students, and developing social contracts (classroom behavior expectations) are a few of the Capturing Kids' Hearts techniques.

Nurturing Self-Esteem

Addressing the social-emotional needs of students is not an extra curriculum. Some educators voice concern that if they expend energy on what might be considered the emotional lives of students (such as students' sense of security, confidence about learning, or their view of the teacher), it will take time away from teaching academic content. It is unfortunate that a belief has emerged in some quarters that nurturing a student's emotional and social well-being is mutually exclusive from reinforcing academic skills.

Dr. Robert Brooks is convinced by his own experience as well as the feedback he has received from numerous educators that ". . . strengthening a student's self-worth is not an 'extra' curriculum that siphons time from teaching academics; if anything, a student's sense of belonging, security, and self-confidence in a classroom provides the scaffolding that bolsters the foundation for enhanced learning, motivation, self-discipline, and caring."

Taking Risks

School can feel like a pretty unsafe place to take risks unless the teacher works deliberately to combat this feeling among students. Giving an incorrect answer in class can be embarrassing, so some students may not choose to share if they are uncertain. These students may have concluded that the price they pay for taking risks and making mistakes is not worth the rewards should they happen to succeed.

However, when you build relationships with your students and demonstrate a sincere interest in them and their learning, the classroom can become a relatively safe place to take a risk. Not only do you get to know your students well, these students become more invested in you and the material that you are teaching. Dr. Robert Brooks states, "Those relationships provide an incredible foundation of trust that allows you to connect emotionally *and* intellectually with your students, and that connection can produce remarkable results."

Sharing stories with your students about risks you have taken yourself— such as learning a new skill that you turned out not to be very good at but enjoyed anyway, or applying for a job you really wanted even though you knew there was lots of competition. Hearing how things you learned and how you grew stronger from taking risks, even when you were unsuccessful, can give students a lot of confidence. After all, look how successful you are now!

Now here's the challenge: Just because your students trust you doesn't mean they are going to trust their classmates. And to truly learn and grow, they are going to need to take emotional and intellectual risks in front of that group.

The best approach is to let your students know that you understand that trying new skills and learning new material can be scary. Let them know that you recognize and appreciate all of their efforts, and that you will insist that students in the class demonstrate this encouraging attitude as well. Remember that boys and girls will often "encourage" each other differently, so allow some latitude in what is acceptable as long as it is obviously not mean. Make it clear that their risk taking will set a positive tone and example in the classroom. Be there to encourage, guide, and help students recover from mistakes. You will also be there to help them celebrate the accomplishments borne of their courage and work.

> *The person who risks nothing, does nothing, has nothing, is nothing and becomes noting. He may avoid suffering and sorrow, but he simply cannot learn and feel and change and grow and love and live.*
>
> —Leo F. Buscaglia

Practical Ideas for Your Classroom

Robert Brooks said, "For some students the only moments of safety, security, and acceptance they experience are in your classroom." The truth of this statement, like all truths, is played out in little things, moments of connection, small practical ideas and activities that are, in the heart of the child, writ quite large.

Let's focus on some specific areas of practicality with ideas and tools.

Helping Students with Disabilities

Positive teacher-student relationships seem to be particularly beneficial for children with disabilities, who are at risk because they don't have the requisite skills for entering kindergarten, or who start school with behavior problems, cognitive difficulties, or social problems. In a study examining the quality of teacher-student relationships among kindergartners with low performance, it was found that those with closer, less conflicted relationships with their teachers were less likely to be retained or placed in special education by the end of the year.

In a 2005 study by Rebecca Silver and her colleagues at the University of Oregon, the researchers found that when children began kindergarten with high levels of acting out, impulsivity, or aggression, a high level of teacher-student closeness correlated to significant decreases in behavior problems by the time those students were in third grade.

A positive teacher-student relationship is what every child needs, but it can be more difficult to forge these relationships with students who exhibit contrary behaviors. Rebecca Silver suggests that understanding students' challenging behaviors can help teachers prevent those behaviors from interfering with successful relationships.

Tips for working with students with disabilities include

- Enhancing awareness of and belief in the abilities of students

- Developing a repertoire of ways to convey the highest possible expectations for students

- Becoming more aware of, and having increased belief in, their own abilities

- Recognizing the importance and power of one-on-one encounters with students

Looping

"Looping" is an essentially simple concept: a teacher moves with his or her students to the next grade level, rather than sending them to another teacher at the end of the school year. Some loops are two consecutive years with the same group of students, while others may spend three or more years with the same group. Despite enthusiastic practitioners, the positive experience of European school systems, and favorable research, looping is still uncommon enough in the United States to be considered innovative.

The available literature points to many benefits of looping. Students change from one grade to the next with a minimum of anxiety. Looping provides children with additional time to build the relationships on which much of their learning depends. Looping can turn parents into supporters and promotes stronger bonding between parents and teachers. Looping essentially adds an extra month of teaching-learning time during the second year when the typical transitional period at the beginning of the year is virtually unnecessary.

There are two potential downsides of looping:

An inappropriate match, or personality conflict, between teacher and student—a situation that can occur in a traditional classroom as well. Such actual problems are rare and can usually be solved by transferring those students to another teacher.

The need to alternate yearly between two different grade level curricula. This, of course, only requires additional work in the first two years as you become familiar with the grade level standards.

Looping does not require the participation of an entire faculty. Looping requires only two willing teachers to make it work. While some schools operate entirely on a looping structure, many schools have a mixture of traditional and looping classrooms. They key is to gain the support of the principal and a potential teaching partner. The ability to forge strong personal connections with students makes looping an attractive option for many classroom teachers.

Mentoring

Mentoring is defined as a one-to-one relationship between a youth and an adult that occurs over a prolonged period of time. Mentoring is not the same as teaching. You can teach thirty students at a time, but you have to mentor one student at a time.

A mentor provides consistent support, guidance, and concrete help to a student who is in need of a positive role model. The goal of mentoring is to help students form a relationship with a caring individual, as well as to gain skills, knowledge, and confidence. Not only will students learn new skills, they will also learn firsthand the importance of collaboration and team spirit. The encouragement they will receive from a supportive mentor will help enhance students' belief in their own abilities.

Sometimes it is possible and appropriate for a teacher to serve as a mentor for a child. Often, there are time constraints that make this more difficult. Therefore, as a classroom teacher, you may wish to actively seek out individuals who might serve as mentors to your students. Older students, community members, and parents can all be recruited to become mentors.

It is especially helpful to find older males to mentor boys, and older females to mentor girls. Positive, same-sex role models give children a picture of who they can be. Once the trusting relationship is established, boys and girls can ask personal questions about growing up that only someone who has literally "walked in their gender shoes" can best answer.

The National Mentoring Partnership (www.mentoring.org/) has an extensive searchable online database of local and regional mentoring programs, which also include information about caring adult programs, volunteer centers, and local mentoring partnerships in communities throughout the United States.

Additional resources include:

1–877- BE A MENTOR

Punch in your zip code to find a mentoring opportunity nearest you!

The National Mentoring Partnership

www.mentoring.org/

Phone: 202–729–4340

The Mentor Resource Center

www.calmentor.ca.gov/

Phone: 800–444–3066

A hundred years from now it will not matter what my bank account was, the sort of house I lived in, or the kind of car I drove. . . . But the world might be a better place because I was important in the life of a child.

—Author unknown

Things You Can Do Right Now!

➡ Start the school year by having everyone—including you—reflect on and share goals, intentions, and aspirations for the year. Be sure to build in time to periodically reflect on those goals and to celebrate milestones!

➡ Invest time during the first two weeks of school in forming individual relationships with your students. For example, invite small groups of students to eat lunch with you, play recess games with the students, ask them about themselves, or write personal notes.

➡ Get to know your students' interests better by having them complete an "Interest Inventory."

➡ Organize non-academic extracurricular activities for students and teachers to participate in together.

➡ Develop disciplinary policies that carry high expectations for students while fostering caring relationships. For example, using mediation strategies as alternatives to punitive discipline.

➡ Genuinely listen to students' concerns and perspectives.

➡ Respond to transgressions gently and with explanations.

➡ Compliment positive behavior. "Catch them being good" regularly. Always reward the behavior you would like to see more of.

➡ Show positive emotions (such as by smiling or being playful) regularly.

➡ Demonstrate a willingness to address the non-academic needs of students.

➡ Show an interest in students' lives outside of school. Get to know a little about the pop culture (such as music, TV shows, and video games) that appeal to your students. This will help you converse with them when they tell you what they like.

➡ Communicate regularly about academic progress and provide your students with specific and timely feedback.

➡ Refuse to accept half-hearted efforts from your students.

➡ Provide encouragement always.

➡ Build a relationship with the parents of your students. They want to know you and want to be confident that they can entrust their son or daughter into your care. By taking interest in their family, you further strengthen the trust that your students and their parents have in you.

➡ Consider attending one extracurricular activity for each of your students during the school year. Often, a few students are playing on the same team or in the same play, so this means fewer events to attend overall.

➡ Ask yourself these questions:

   ➡ How do I help each student to feel welcome in my classroom?

   ➡ What choices do I provide my students so that they develop a sense of ownership for their education?

   ➡ Do I incorporate and teach problem-solving skills in my activities so that students have an opportunity to learn how to make informed decisions?

   ➡ Do I discipline more as a form of punishment or as a way of teaching self-discipline? That is, do I involve students in helping to create some of the rules and consequences in the classroom so that they experience greater responsibility for their own behavior?

   ➡ Do I convey from the first day of school that mistakes are part of the learning process, that mistakes are expected and accepted and not to be feared?

   ➡ *Would I want to be in my class???*

WRAPPING UP THE MAIN POINTS

- Building a positive teacher-student relationship is a key step in creating a caring and safe learning community.

- A strong predictor of student success is the relationships students have with their teachers. Studies have shown decreased retention and special education referrals for students who enjoy a higher degree of closeness with their teachers.

- All children need a significant adult in their lives to whom they can go to, talk to, and rely on. Children often identify this special adult as their teacher.

- Students with disabilities have a more pronounced need for a strong teacher-student relationship in order to experience success at school.

- Part of a strong teacher-student relationship is trust. Students must be able to trust that the teacher will ensure a caring community among students so that the classroom environment is safe for risk taking.

What the teacher is, is more important than what he teaches.

—Soren Kierkegaard

Building Character

The Foundation for Learning and Life

9

The function of education is to teach one to think intensively and to think critically. . . Intelligence plus character—that is the goal of true education.

—Martin Luther King Jr.

IMAGINE that you walk into an elementary school where everyone is courteous and helpful to one another. Students say "please" and "thank you" in the lunch line. They stop in the hallway to pick up a stray piece of trash. They help a friend who's feeling sad and they are cooperative and attentive in class. The teachers work together collaboratively and respectfully. Parents and community members support the work of the school in meaningful ways. Support staff smile and greet students by name. Sound idealistic? Perhaps—but a positive school climate is within reach. Character education goes to the very bedrock of the school. It has the power to change the climate of a classroom or a school in very real ways.

If we are to reach real peace in this world . . . we shall have to begin with children.

—Mohandas Gandhi

Why Character Education Works

YOU are a character educator. You work with students who observe, learn from, and emulate you. You teach through your actions and words. Students learn what you expect, the kinds of behaviors that you tolerate, and the deeds that go rewarded. This reality is inescapable. Many teachers, however, don't have a systematic plan for teaching character assets in their classrooms. Sure, teachers may have a set of classroom rules and a system of rewards and consequences, but character education goes far beyond that, encompassing every single thing you do that influences the character of the kids you teach.

The intent of character education in schools is to foster personal and civic virtues such as kindness, respect, responsibility, integrity, and effort among all members of the school community. Character education is an ongoing long-term effort, not a quick-fix program. Character education is all about helping young people to be the best that they can be in a school environment where certain virtues, or "character assets," as they are commonly known, are expected, taught, celebrated, modeled, and practiced. A strong schoolwide character asset program can create a pervasive sense of "this is how we are at this school" if the assets are woven deeply into the fabric of the life of the school.

Positive character can be described in many ways, including the inward motivation to do what is right even when no one is watching. It is not only a school skill—it is a life skill that can mean the difference between success and failure for students. Character education can teach students to make the right choices when it comes to the decisions in their lives, from homework to school attendance, from classroom behavior to bullying. As a youngster, this may be the choice to turn in a dollar bill found on the playground or to help a friend who's feeling down. Later in life, these same students will rely on their character to make potentially life-changing decisions.

Schools and teachers today are focused on raising standards of academic achievement as measured by district and state assessments and NCLB. However, as we consider the world in which we live, we understand the importance of helping students to learn much more than the subjects they study. Appropriate environments, activities, the arts, and service projects can help students to learn responsibility, compassion, integrity, civility, leadership, and cooperation. These and other elements of healthy, well-developed character can be learned by example and opportunities to exercise them.

As Dr. Thomas Lickona, author of *Educating for Character*, states: "Moral education is not a new idea. It is, in fact, as old as education itself. Down through history, in countries all over the world, education has had two great goals: to help young people become smart and to help them become good." Good character is not formed automatically; it is developed over time through a sustained process of teaching, example, learning, and practice.

Since character is seemingly an inner trait, how might we recognize character in ourselves or others? When it comes to character, good or bad, we generally accept that it is observable in one's conduct. Character is different from values in that values are orientations or beliefs. Values include both what we know and how we feel about what we know. Character, on the other hand, involves putting our values into action.

? DID YOU KNOW? There Are Three Domains of Character

Cognition *(thinking):* refers to the process of coming to know and understand; the process of encoding, storing, processing, and retrieving information. It is generally associated with the question of "what": What happened? What is going on now? What is the meaning of the information?

Affect *(feeling):* refers to the emotional interpretation of perceptions, information, or knowledge. It is generally associated with one's attachment (positive or negative, to people, objects, ideas, and so on), and asks the question, "How do I feel about this information?"

Conation *(acting):* refers to the connection of knowledge and affect to behavior, and is associated with the issue of "why." It is the personal, intentional, planful, deliberate, goal-oriented, or striving component of motivation, the proactive (as opposed to reactive or habitual) aspect of behavior. It is closely associated with the concept of volition, the use of will, or the freedom to make choices about what to do.

Conation is very important when addressing issues of human learning because it includes behaviors related to self-concept, self-reflection, self-determination, and setting goals. Conation is what drives motivation, decisions about what to do and not do, and the development of a plan of action. Helping students to understand and regulate each of these components can aid them in developing the positive character traits that will enhance success in school and in life. Character education brings benefits for children in both the social-emotional realm and the academic realm.

In a 2003 study called *The Relationship of Character Education Implementation and Academic Achievement in Elementary Schools*, Benninga, Berkowitz, Kuehn, and Smith explored links between character education programs and improvements in academic achievement in elementary schools. The researchers compared scores on a rubric measuring traits of character education programs in more than six hundred California schools to a numeric indicator that summarized the results of various statewide assessments. The team found that schools with the strongest character education scores tended to have higher academic scores by a small but statistically significant margin.

The team also identified three program attributes that had the strongest links with academic achievement:

- A school's ability to ensure a clean and safe physical environment
- Evidence that parents and teachers modeled and promoted good character education
- Opportunities for students to contribute in meaningful ways to the school and its community

The Principles of Good Character

Your actions speak louder than words.

Do the right thing even when no one is watching.

Don't let others' bad behavior serve as a model for you. Choose to do better.

One person can make a big difference in this life.

You are defined by your choices. Make good ones!

Good character makes you a better person and makes the world a better place.

In the Students' Words

After a classroom discussion about applying effort and learning from mistakes, these three third graders wrote the following pieces:

I've learned that life is hard and you shouldn't just cry about it. It's your responsibility for turning in your homework. You're the only one that can make you happy. You can be who you want to be, you choose who you want to be. Do what's right instead of pouting about it. You can do good instead of bad. Stand up to your problems, don't run away from them.

———————

When life puts you down, stand up to it. Sometimes life can act like your friend and sometimes a bully. When life acts like a bully, you don't just whine about it. Get over it! One thing that will give you a better life is don't use your tears to get someone to solve your problem for you. Another thing is never say you can't do it. Another thing is never let life get you down. Those are some ways to have a better life. You'll learn some more ways as you grow up.

———————

I've learned that you can just sit thinking about your problems or you can be positive and accept that life is sometimes difficult and not always fair. You have to be responsible about what you choose, and it's very important not to blame somebody else. Responsibility for what you choose to be like is very important.

To educate a person in mind and not in morals is to educate a menace to society.

—Theodore Roosevelt

Common Teacher Questions and Concerns

"Who decides what virtues or character assets will be taught?"

In collaboration with parents, teachers, and community members, each school can tailor character education to meet the unique needs of the school and local community. In general, character education focuses on the core ethical values which form the foundation of a democratic society: respect, responsibility, trustworthiness, caring, justice, fairness, and citizenship. If character education is not a systematic, schoolwide initiative at your school, you can still identify character assets to serve as the foundation for how your classroom community does its work together.

"Should I teach specific character education lessons or can it be more infused with the curriculum?"

Character education lessons can indeed be stand-alone lessons in developing good character. However, the foundation of character education should permeate everything about your students' school experience—and consistently be supported at all levels, including administrators, teachers, support staff, custodians, and volunteers. Everyone that comes in contact with students is teaching character education and setting an example.

Recognizing that there is limited time in the school day, educators must typically integrate activities that can develop the character traits into an already crowded curriculum. Therefore, many teachers choose to infuse character education into all aspects of the curriculum—and it's a natural and easy fit! For example, fiction and non-fiction stories have protagonists and antagonists. History is not simply a timeline of events; rather, it is a chronicle of humans and the choices and decisions they have made. Science can provide opportunities to discuss what students believe about a variety of ethical topics. The academic curriculum itself provides multiple opportunities to discuss the virtues of responsibility, respect, kindness, self-control, effort, integrity, and more.

"Where can I find resources for teaching character in my classroom?"

There are a number of helpful resources on the Web, many of which include actual lesson plans to teach certain character assets. The following are a few sites that you might wish to check out:

Character Counts! (www.charactercounts.org) is a voluntary partnership which supports character education nationally. The six pillars of character identified by the coalition include respect, responsibility, trustworthiness, caring, fairness, and citizenship. A variety of resource materials are available, along with training sessions and awards recognition.

Parts of the Brain Involved in Developing Character

As we've already discussed, character has three domains—what we know, how we feel, and how we choose to act. Each of these functions requires complex neurological work involving many different areas of the brain. Below are just a few of the key brain areas associated with *knowing, feeling* and *acting.*

Cerebral cortex: is only a 2–4 mm thick surface on the brain, yet it plays a central role in many complex brain functions including memory, attention, perceptual awareness, language, consciousness, and "thinking!"

Frontal lobe: organizes and arranges information; coordinates planning, problem solving, judgment, the production of language, and the focusing of attention.

Limbic system: a group of interconnected deep brain structures involved in a number of functions, including emotion, motivation, and behavior.

Right ventral striatum: a part of the brain responsible for calculating risk and reward. This area of the brain helps people summon motivation for a task.

The Giraffe Project (www.giraffe.org) challenges participants to "stick their necks out" for good character. The program offers examples of heroes who stuck their necks out for the care and concern of others. Students explore the difference between being a "hero" and a "celebrity" and work toward developing a caring local community. Resource materials are available for students in K–12.

The Character Education Partnership (www.character.org) was founded in 1993 as a national nonpartisan coalition for character education. The CEP recognizes National Schools of Character that serve as models of exemplary character education practice in the country. Go to their Resources link to find a character education blog, book lists, excellent background information, and "toolkits" for setting up and evaluating a character education program.

Center for the 4th and 5th Rs (www.cortland.edu/character) is sponsored by the State University of New York College at Cortland. It provides book lists, professional development opportunities, assessment tools, and a *12-Point Comprehensive Approach to Character Education.*

"My school hasn't adopted a schoolwide character education program. What can I do?"

Character education can be taken on by an individual teacher or by an entire school. Of course, it is much better if character education is woven into every aspect of school life with common language and expectations that everyone in the school knows and is committed to. If your school does not have a formal character education program in place already, this might be an opportunity for teacher leadership. Consider talking to your school principal and forming a committee of teachers, parents, and other staff members to explore the possibility of a schoolwide program. If this is not possible, you can still create a culture of caring and positive character traits in your own classroom or on your grade level team.

A Word About Television Violence

Since the 1950s, literally thousands of studies have been conducted to determine whether or not there is a link between exposure to media violence and violent behavior. All but eighteen of these studies have determined that the answer is: Yes.

Take a look at the following questions and consider whether or not television helps or hinders efforts toward developing positive character in children. Consider sharing this list of questions with parents as they partner with you to raise children of character.

- How many violent acts, including murder, do children see on television every day?

- What percentage of prime time programming contains violence?

- Are the perpetrators of violence on TV punished for their violent acts? How often?

- How often is violence on TV presented in the context of "fun" or as a "good way to get what you want?"

- How much violence do you see in G-rated movies and videos? This includes animated feature films and movies targeting children as the audience.

- How often do TV and movies make it "OK" for the good guy to use physical violence to "get the bad guy?"

- How often do you see young children emulating what they see on TV and in movies in their play with each other?

- How desensitized do children become from exposure to such consistent messages of violence?

- How many studies have shown a direct link between watching violence on TV or playing violent video games and children's aggressive behavior?

- How many teenage boys who end up as adult offenders watched a lot of TV growing up?

Research provides answers to all these questions—answers that should be seriously considered as parents and teachers make choices about exposing children to any media. The research is readily available online using any search engine. Check it out!

The Critical Role of the School Staff

A review of research shows that the quality of relationships among teachers and other staff members is a major factor in the development of student character. An atmosphere of adult harmony is vitally important. Schools that effectively assist pupil character development are filled with adults who are consistent, compassionate, fair minded, and who practice what they preach.

In *Moral Teachers, Moral Students,* Rick Weissbourd eloquently describes the adult's complex role at school:

Educators influence students' moral development not only by being good role models—important as that is—but also by what they bring to their relationships with students day to day: their ability to appreciate students' perspectives and to disentangle them from their own, their ability to admit and learn from moral error, their moral energy and idealism, their generosity, and their ability to help students develop moral thinking without shying away from their own moral authority. That level of influence makes being an adult in a school a profound moral challenge.

Most people say that it is the intellect which makes a great scientist. They are wrong: it is character.

—Albert Einstein

The Personal Benefits of Caring and Compassion

Most runners are familiar with the "runner's high," but have you ever heard of a "helper's high?" That is what Allan Luks, co-author of *The Healing Power of Doing Good,* calls the feeling of physiological and psychological exhilaration experienced by many people when they help others. Of course, we don't seek to help others for personal gain; however, it is interesting to note that there are both emotional and physical benefits associated with being of service to others.

Children are natural helpers. Many of them love to help the teacher, help other students or younger children, and participate in community service. Children usually get very motivated about collecting money to help victims of a tragedy or to send care packages to overseas troops.

With an understanding of the research regarding the helper's high phenomenon, there is an opportunity to talk with children about the healing powers of compassion. After a community service activity or a classroom buddies activity, consider giving children the opportunity to reflect deeply about the experience, both in terms of the benefit given and the benefit received. Perhaps they can come to understand that, through being compassionate to others, we add value and meaning to our own lives.

Character, in the long run, is the decisive factor in the life of an individual and of nations alike.

—Theodore Roosevelt

Anti-Bullying Programs & Resources

An essential part of every classroom, school, and character education program is systematic and direct instruction to students about bullying.

In fact, many states require schools to have some kind of anti-bullying program in place. Creating a culture of "no bullying" will be most effective when there is a schoolwide initiative in place that includes the use of common language and expectations about bullying.

Character education is truly the proactive approach to bullying. If students understand the meaning of character traits such as respect, integrity, kindness, and empathy, they will understand that you cannot demonstrate these traits and bully at the same time. It has to be one or the other; it can't be both. If everyone agrees to live by the character creed of your classroom or school, then bullying won't happen. Of course, bullying situations still occur from time to time but, when they do, you will be able to return to the language you've used when teaching the students about character: How did that person feel? How might you have shown respect? What is the most responsible thing to do at this point?

Below is a partial list of the many resources that are available to parents and teachers on the topic of bullying:

Bullyproofing Your School (www.ccsd.k12.co.us/dist_info/safeschools/prevention/bullyproofing.html)

No-Bullying Program (www.hazelden.org)

Schoolwide Prevention of Bullying (www.nwrel.org/request/dec01/school-wide.html)

Stamp Out Bullying (www.no-bully.com/teachers.html)

Steps to Respect (www.cfchildren.org/strf/strf/strindex/)

The Kindness Campaign (www.thekindnesscampaign.org)

The Incredible Years (www.incredibleyears.com/)

Children's Books That Teach About Character

Many children's books have a moral or a lesson that can be used to spark an excellent discussion in the classroom. Many book lists have been created that serve to align specific children's books with the different character traits. Your librarian will be able to recommend wonderful books in a variety of genres offering lessons in all areas of character development. Additionally, searching the Internet will produce wonderful lists of recommended books in the area of character development.

But if you ask what is the good of education in general, the answer is easy: that education makes good men, and that good men act nobly.

—Plato

Practical Ideas for Your Classroom

General Classroom Practice

➡ Praise your students' effort and striving, not their ability.

➡ Everyone needs to develop a mission statement as one way to help think about one's priorities. This statement provides an opportunity for the individual to explicitly consider and state important values and beliefs. Do this activity with your students. Have them ask themselves:

  ➡ Who are the most important people in your life?

  ➡ What qualities would you like to be remembered for?

  ➡ Think of a favorite friend. What qualities does he or she possess that you would also like to have?

  ➡ What is one word to describe yourself?

➡ Develop a "Code of Ethics" with your students, and post it prominently in your classroom. Have students share this code with their parents.

➡ If your classroom or school has identified certain character assets, have students create large posters with statements and phrases about what each asset might look like when it is being put in action. For example, a poster on Respect might have statements such as, "Saying please or thank you," "Saying I'm sorry when I hurt someone," "Doing what the teacher asks me to do." A Responsibility poster might include, "Do my homework and turn it in on time," "Make sure I do my classroom job everyday," and "Use my class time well."

➡ Hold regular classroom meetings. These fifteen-minute meetings have a flexible agenda in which students can bring up things that are going well and things that are not going well within their classroom community. Certain ground rules apply, such as not "naming names" and respecting the need for confidentiality. Classroom meetings give students an opportunity to talk about problems in a proactive way, acknowledge acts of kindness, and engage in discussion about good choices and good character.

➡ Encourage students to identify a charity or in-school need, collect donations, and help administer the distribution of funds. Alternatively, invite student volunteers to clean up their community. With parental support, encourage students to build a community playground, pick up litter, rake leaves, plant trees, paint a mural, remove graffiti, or clean up a local park or beach. Classes could "adopt a hallway," shelve misplaced books, plant flowers, for example. Post signs identifying the caretakers.

➡ Ensure that the school's recognition system covers both character and academics.

➡ Consistently prohibit gossip and, when appropriate, address or discuss its damaging consequences.

➡ Use morning announcements, school or classroom bulletin boards, or the school newsletter to highlight the various accomplishments—particularly character-oriented ones—of students and faculty members.

➡ In physical education and sports programs, place a premium on good sportsmanship. Participation in sports should provide good habits for the life beyond sports.

➡ Hang pictures of heroes and heroines in classrooms and halls. Include appropriate explanatory text.

➡ Have your students publicly recognize the work of the school's "unsung heroes" who keep the school running: the custodians, repairmen, secretaries, cafeteria workers, and volunteers. They could write them thank-you notes or even invite them as special guests to an appreciation assembly of students and staff.

➡ Don't underestimate the power of stories to build a child's moral imagination. Read aloud to students daily.

➡ Conduct literature discussions—even in the youngest grades. General questions could include: What did this book make you think about or feel? Tell me about (a character's name)—what kind of person was he? Why do you think the author wrote this book—what did she want to say to the reader?

➡ Build empathy in literature and social studies classes by teaching children to "put themselves in the shoes" of the people they are reading about or studying.

➡ Read and discuss biographies from all subject areas. Help students identify the person's core or defining characteristics.

➡ Teach students to write thoughtful letters: thank-you notes, letters to public officials, letters to the editor, and so on.

➡ Lead by example. Pick up the piece of paper in the hall. Leave the classroom clean. Say, "Thank you."

➡ Admit mistakes and seek to make amends. Expect and encourage students to do likewise.

➡ Follow through. Do what you say you will do. For example, administer tests when they are scheduled; don't cancel at the last minute after students have prepared.

➡ Give students sufficient and timely feedback when you evaluate their work. This demonstrates to students that their work matters and that teachers take a stake in their improvement and success.

➡ Develop a list of suggested readings and resources in character education and share it with parents.

➡ In your classroom newsletters, include a message about character in addition to academic goals and projects.

In the Content Areas

➡ In science, address with each unit (when appropriate) the ethical considerations of that field of study. Students need to see that morality and ethics are not confined to the humanities.

➡ In social studies, examine the responsibilities of the citizen. What can students do right now to build the habits of responsible citizenship?

➡ Have students do a major paper on a living public figure ("My Personal Hero") focusing on the moral achievements and virtues of the individual. First, do the groundwork of helping them to understand what constitutes a particularly noble life. Celebrate the birthdays of heroes and heroines with discussion of their accomplishments. Tell your students who your heroes are and why you chose them.

➡ Show students the cover of the book *Now One Foot, Now the Other* by Tomie dePaola. Have students predict what the book is going to be about based on the cover. Read the book to your students. Discuss the actions of Bobby and his grandfather throughout the story. How did their relationship change? How did it stay the same? Introduce students to the word "compassion" and explain that compassion is helping others and putting their needs before your own. Ask them to explain how Bobby showed compassion to his grandfather. Explain that students will be responsible for finding a picture of someone showing compassion in a newspaper or magazine at home and bring it in to school. Send home a letter to explain the assignment to parents. Once students have brought in their picture, ask them to glue it to a piece of construction paper and write a sentence to go with the picture explaining how the characters in the picture are showing compassion. Finally, give each student a piece of construction or drawing paper to create a compassionate get-well card for Bobby's grandfather.

➡ Read *Too Many Tamales* aloud to the class. When you get to the point in the story when the girl decides to play with her mother's ring, ask the students to predict what will happen to the girl or to the ring.

　➡ After finishing the story, ask the children to tell you what the problem was in the story. (Maria lost her mother's ring when she wasn't supposed to be playing with it.)

　➡ What did Maria do to solve the problem?

　➡ Do you think that was a good solution to the problem? Why or why not?

➡ Was Maria honest with her mother at first?

➡ What happened when Maria told her mother the truth?

➡ What might have happened if Maria had told her mother the truth when she first realized it was gone?

➡ Help students acquire the power of discernment—including the ability to judge the truth, worth, and bias of what is presented on the TV, radio, and the Internet.

➡ Invite graduates of your school to return and talk about their experience in the next stage of life. Ask them to discuss what habits or virtues could make the transition to middle school successful. What bad habits or vices cause problems?

➡ During election years, encourage students to research candidates' positions, listen to debates, participate in voter registration drives, and encourage their parents to vote.

➡ Discipline and classroom management should concentrate on problem-solving rather than rewards and punishments.

WRAPPING UP THE MAIN POINTS

- Character education provides the foundation for a safe and civil environment that is conducive for learning.

- The intent of character education in schools is to foster personal and civic virtues such as kindness, respect, responsibility, integrity, and effort among all members of the school community.

- Character is a combination of what we *know,* what we *feel,* and how we choose to *act.* It is the process of putting our values into action.

- Character education is most effective when there is a schoolwide initiative that is supported by a collaborative staff.

- Systematic and sequential instruction in the area of bullying is an essential component of any character education program.

What lies behind us and what lies before us are small matters compared to what lies within us.

—Ralph Waldo Emerson

The Home Stretch

Getting Parents and Teachers on the Same Page

10

*Making the decision to have a child is momentous. It is to decide
forever to have your heart go walking around outside your body.*
—Elizabeth Stone

THE home-school partnership is an important ingredient in every
child's academic, behavioral, and social progress. Without ongoing communication, a child's primary caretakers and teachers
don't know how they can work together to support the child's development. Parents come in as many shapes and forms as your students, but an
effective teacher can implement strategies to maximize opportunities for
parent involvement from all kinds of parents and, in doing so, increase
students' success.

Why Home-School Partnerships Work

Parents' involvement in their children's education is widely considered to
have many positive benefits for children's development and academic performance and for improving schools. The complexity of the relationship
between families and schools defies a simple definition. Parental involvement looks different based on the family's composition, the work responsibilities of the parents, the language background of the parents, and the degree
to which the school is a welcoming place for parents, as well as the parents'
perceptions of school based on their own school experiences.

At a minimum, parental support entails ensuring that children attend
school regularly, arrive on time, and come ready to learn. "Ready to learn"
should include being well rested, well fed, and free from unnecessary stress.
It also means assistance from parents if classroom behavior problems emerge.
The interdependency of home and school is particularly important at the primary grade level, where the school is an extension of the family. If learning

is to occur, the trust developed between a parent and child during the first years of life must be transferred to school staff. Teachers need parents to help their children understand that the teacher has a special role in the child's life, much like that of an extended family member.

In a study conducted by the National Center for Education Statistics, school-aged children are more likely to get good grades, enjoy school, and participate in extracurricular activities if their parents have a high level of involvement in the school. Also, students with involved parents have lower rates of retention, suspension, and expulsion compared to students whose parents have low levels of school involvement. In fact, parental involvement has a higher correlation to student success than family income or education.

When conflicts do arise, families may feel that their interests are not fully taken into account by teachers. At other times, parents may feel that educators talk down to them or speak in educational jargon they do not understand. Teachers, on their part, can become frustrated by a lack of parental involvement; the nature of some parents' involvement may also cause difficulties. To make the home-school partnership work, educators need to be willing to recognize the extent of this disconnect as they plan for involving families in their children's education. To that end, communication— open, direct, ongoing, and cordial—is the key.

There are no quick fixes or easy answers to building home-school relationships and partnerships. The answer lies in helping parents understand their critical role, a willingness of educators to rethink and reinvent the role of parents and school-family relationships, and the cooperation of the entire community.

> *The pessimist sees difficulty in every opportunity. The optimist sees opportunity in every difficulty.*
>
> —Winston Churchill

Effective Communication with Parents

What do parents say that they want most in their child's teacher? When we talk with parents, we hear them appealing for good communication skills in their children's teachers. The parent of a first grader shares, "I appreciate it when I get frequent communication either through notes or a phone call or e-mail. I want to know if my child is having problems before they become serious. It's also nice to hear the good things that are happening."

Parents frequently comment on how hard it can be to stay on top of upcoming activities, events, and curriculum. Information from school is the primary means parents have to understand their children's level of success or failure. Research supports that home-school communication is among the most important factors in developing strong relationships between teachers and families.

Parents receive information from the school in a variety of ways, including school or classroom newsletters, flyers, weekly notes or folders, school district mailings, phone calls, e-mails, formal parent-teacher conferences, quick conversations "on the fly," Back-to-School nights, principal-led talks, and school tours. Formal and informal means of communication work together to shape a parent's experience and, in turn, color his or her impression of the teacher and the school.

Good communication starts with getting clarity about your purpose, because there are a multitude of reasons that teachers communicate with parents. Being clear about the purpose of the communication can help you stay on track during your meeting. Consider, too, that parents also have desired outcomes. Do they want to ask for help, share information, or follow up with you? If you are uncertain of the parent's goals, consider establishing this up front. The purposes for communication include:

- *Informing.* Teachers need to communicate for the purpose of sharing information about the curriculum, the discipline policy, grading system, or other aspects of the classroom management or instruction.

- *Follow-up.* Teachers need to contact parents to remind them of an event or to close the loop on a prior discussion. Teachers might follow-up about a child's attendance or remind parents about an upcoming event or conference.

- *Asking for help.* Teachers ask parents about strategies that work particularly well at home and might be tried at school.

- *Sharing information.* The type of communication involves sharing goals, thoughts, and concerns to give a total picture of what's going on at school.

- *Informal exchange.* This reciprocal dialogue typically involves chatting with no specific agenda, sharing impressions, finding out what's on the parent's mind.

- *Active listening.* Perhaps the most important type of communication, this involves listening and paying attention. Listening to parents' concerns and also allowing them to have an agenda honors their contributions and wisdom.

As important as home-school communication is, a number of obstacles exist for both teachers and parents. Teachers face significant time limitations during their day. Their class schedule may make it more difficult to schedule meetings during parents' available times. Parents may have work commitments that make it difficult or impossible for the parent to meet or take phone calls during work hours; parents may also have a language barrier or lack transportation to get to the school. Other parents—due to family composition, socioeconomic status, or other factors—may feel uncomfortable in the school setting or may feel that the school holds negative stereotypes of them.

In all communication, but especially problem-based conversations or meetings, it is helpful to plan ahead with a clear sense of the desired outcome. Remember also that communication is 80 percent nonverbal and just 20 percent verbal. Language, facial and body expression, and pitch and tone of voice, are all ways of transmitting a message. Although most communication occurs spontaneously, the following communication skills can be helpful in all situations: (1) identifying the goal and reason for the communication, (2) considering one's audience, and (3) choosing a communication approach that opens rather than blocks a two-way conversation.

In addition to crafting a clear message, teachers should be sure to inform parents of all the lines of communication that are available to them. It's easy to assume that parents know how or when to contact you, but that may not always be the case. Therefore, it's best to provide parents with a list of communication methods—you may even want to suggest that they keep the note on the fridge or somewhere else for easy reference. The goal is to make it as easy as possible. Below is an example of two different communication tip sheets:

COMMUNICATING WITH MR. TEACHER

- *Phone:* 212-555-2121; I am available before school (7:00–8:00 A.M.) most mornings and after school (2:45–3:45 P.M.) on Mondays and Wednesdays. You may also wish to call me during my planning time which is 10:35–11:15 A.M. daily. If you cannot call during those times, please leave a voicemail message and I will call you back promptly.

- *E-mail:* mr.teacher@ourschool.org; please feel free to e-mail me any time. I do my best to return e-mails the same day; however, sometimes I cannot get to them until the end of the day or the next morning. I also check e-mail on the weekend.

- *Written note:* Please send handwritten notes in your child's home-school folder to prevent them from getting lost in the bottom of a backpack.

- *Parent-teacher conferences:* Formal conferences are held in October and February. You will be notified when it is time to sign up and I do like to have 100 percent attendance from my students' parents.

- *Scheduled meeting:* Sometimes it is necessary to schedule a meeting outside of the formal parent-teacher conferences to discuss a particular issue, concern, or problem that has come up. These meetings can be initiated either by you or me. Please call if you feel the need to meet and I will do the same.

The following sheet may be a helpful tool in determining the parents' preferred methods for being contacted by you. Keeping these handy in a binder at both home and school will help you be more efficient with your time. You may also wish to develop a parent contact log sheet to keep track of the content, date, time and outcome of your parent contacts.

Home-School Communication Information

Student's name: _____

Family member #1: _____   Relation to student: _____

Home phone: _____   Work phone: _____

Cell phone: _____   E-mail address: _____

How would you prefer to be contacted? _____ Home _____ Work _____ Cell phone _____ E-mail

When would you prefer to be contacted (days and times)

_____

If you do not have access to phone or e-mail, how may I contact you?

_____

Family member #2: _____   Relation to student: _____

Home phone: _____   Work phone: _____

Cell phone: _____   E-mail address: _____

How would you prefer to be contacted? _____ Home _____ Work _____ Cell phone _____ E-mail

When would you prefer to be contacted (days and times)

_____

If you do not have access to phone or e-mail, how may I contact you?

_____

When the elephants fight, the grass gets trampled.

—African proverb

Even in the most difficult of circumstances, it is important to remember that parents are our partners, not our adversaries. When educators and parents become adversaries, it is the child who suffers. It is not always an easy task to develop positive parent-teacher relationships, especially when a child is demonstrating academic or behavioral difficulties in school, but it is an important goal to work toward. As the professionals, teachers are the ones who must show restraint and demonstrate professionalism, even in the face of unwarranted criticism or negativity. Communicating with parents in a positive way enhances teachers' relationships with parents and, most important, has a beneficial effect on the learning and motivation of the students.

Are You Talking To Mom or Dad?

Another dimension to consider when you are approaching a parent conference is this: are you talking to mom, dad, or both parents? The dynamics of gender enter this interaction as well. Mothers will tend to approach the conference from a relationships perspective: Do you like her child? Does her child think you like him or her? If there are problems in the relationship between the child and teacher, mom will want to make things better for her child. Mothers are just as concerned as fathers are about their children being successful in school, but may focus more on how the relationship with the teacher and school might be affecting the child's performance.

Dad, on the other hand, will tend to be more focused on how to improve his child's performance or behavior in order for his child to become a stronger student. Performance will be more important, from the male perspective, than feelings. What specifically does he need to do to help his child become task proficient and meet the goals for success in the classroom?

So, how should you as the teacher approach issues with these two perspectives in mind? First, with mom, share information about what her child is doing well. Make sure she knows that you like her child and want to help her child be successful. Take a little more time building rapport with mom before you dive into the problem area to start looking for solutions. When you do address problems, make mom a member of the team helping to solve the problem in a way that will make things better for her child. If the problem you are addressing involves emotional content, mom can be a lot of help in working toward solutions.

With dad, you might want to take a bit more of a bottom-line approach. Again, start off sharing some positives about his child, but then get down to business. Enlist dad's help in working on solutions. Be specific about how dad might help with structure, especially if the child's problem is task completion and attention to detail. What "tools" might you recommend that dad can help provide to improve his child's performance? Set some time-sensitive goals and decide, together, on one or two steps to implement right away to work toward the goals.

With both mom and dad, remember to focus on the behavior, whether performance or social, that you want to address. Parents often see their children as extensions of themselves, and any perceived attitude that the child is "not OK" may well be received as a message that the parent is "not OK" either. Sometimes parents need as much support to be successful parents as their children do to be successful students. Make the parents your ally by becoming part of their team, in addition to offering an invitation for them to become part of yours.

The whole idea of compassion is based on a keen awareness of the interdependence of all these living beings, which are all part of one another, and all involved in one another.

—Thomas Merton

Working with Diverse Families

As we've learned, there can be a number of barriers to parental involvement in school. For families with a different composition or language background, families of color, or families living in poverty, the barriers can be even greater. These parents, however, can be extremely helpful to the teacher as "cultural informants"—that is, they can help interpret the child's behavior through the context of the child's culture or experiences. For example, a child of color may be resistant to coming to school because of racial exclusion on the playground. Another child may become sullen upon learning of a class field trip for fear that his parents cannot afford the admission fee. Another child may act out during a lesson about families because she does not want to talk about her own family—for example, a household with two moms or two dads. Because parental involvement can improve a building's psychological climate and student's academic performance, it is essential to make the extra efforts needed to bring diverse families into the fold.

Teachers' attitudes toward their students significantly shape the level of expectations they hold for their students' learning, how they treat their students, and what students ultimately learn. Understanding how traditional male and female roles within a culture can influence a child's academic performance is important too. Culturally aware teachers respect students and families as individuals and believe that students from diverse backgrounds are equally capable of meeting high learning standards. Holding all students accountable for high academic standards and allowing students to share and draw upon their cultural practices are ways of honoring the strengths that each child brings to the classroom.

Using Technology

Because so many families nowadays have two working parents, it can be more difficult to communicate with them and get them involved with the school. Technology, however, offers some incredible mechanisms for communication that, in some cases, expand it beyond what we ever thought possible!

An up-to-date school Web site can provide families with a wealth of information, including online school newsletters, lunch menus, grade-level curriculum, achievement data, and school improvement reports. Post digital pictures of school or classroom events and—voila!—parents can see what's going on and feel like they are part of the action. What about a Podcast of a school assembly? Make a digital audio or video recording, post it to the Web site and parents (and grandparents), no matter where they are, will be able to tune in to hear a school event or performance.

Consider offering parents the ability to sign up for parent-teacher conferences online through your classroom or school Web site. Given that some parents may not have Internet access, it is prudent to also offer the traditional paper-and-pencil mechanism for signing up. For working parents, however, it can be very difficult to come to school to sign up and, by the time they do, they may have slimmer pickings in terms of conference times. If you have a volunteer webmaster at your school (a great way to get a technologically-savvy parent involved), have him or her design an online conference sign-up tool for you or the whole school. It can even be programmed to send a reminder e-mail automatically to the parents with the date and time of their conference.

Technology can also be harnessed to manage and increase your parent volunteerism. The volunteer management online tool, PTO Manager, allows parents to enter their areas of interest for volunteering. Once the database has been built, committee chairs and teachers can search for the needed volunteers. For example, if you are a kindergarten teacher and want volunteers for gardening help, you can search the database using certain filters which produce a list of green thumbs. PTO Manager generates a list of all the people who expressed interest in helping in that area, as well as their phone numbers and email addresses. PTO Manager is available for a fee at www.ptomanager.com.

There are a number of other online tools that serve a variety of helpful functions. All support teachers in creating open lines of communication and building a strong home-school partnership. You might want to check out:

Blackboard (www.blackboard.com/)

> Blackboard offers free course space to classroom teachers through the CourseSites box at the bottom of the main page. Follow the steps to set up a virtual classroom where students and parents can come to work and meet online.

Bullwhip (www.fhs.net/FHSWeb.nsf/Home)

> Bullwhip offers a suite of free services that include a discussion board, class news postings, a class calendar, document sharing, online surveys, and a mailing list all free and easy to use.

eGroups (www.egroups.com/)

> This service allows you to set up your own mailing list for your school. Simply create a group name, place it in an appropriate group category, and then indicate the preferences for how it will work. This free service can host groups with membership in the tens through the thousands.

LightSpan (www.lightspan.com/)

> Lightspan offers free services for teachers, students, and parents, including a place to build a free classroom Web page.

Talking it Over (http://family.go.com/Features/family_1998_08/nwfm/nwfm88ten/)

> Family.go.com offers an overview of the "ten commandments" of communication between parent and teacher. Jennifer Maienza presents the suggestions for parents, setting the tone for constructive conferences and teacher-parent collaboration throughout the school year.

Using E-mail

E-mail can be an extremely convenient way for busy teachers and parents to touch base. Not only are you free of having to make contacts at specific times, it provides both of you a written record of the message, as well as the date and the time. Be sure to determine which families have access to e-mail and whether or not they prefer it. Also, keep in mind that e-mail eliminates a lot of nonverbal input, which is an important part of communication between teachers and parents, especially moms. It's a lot easier for mom to misinterpret an e-mail because she isn't able to pick up any of the peripheral sensory data that would accompany a face-to-face meeting.

Also remember that e-mails are permanent—they can be printed out and brought up, verbatim, long after they are sent!

Homework

There's probably not a parent out there that hasn't used a teacher's name in vain at least once at 10:30 p.m. on a school night. There can be heel-dragging, lost worksheets, parent-child meltdowns, and last-minute runs to the corner store for poster board. In fact, homework itself can become a bone of contention that can strain the home-school relationship, not to mention the parent-child relationship.

Communicating with parents early in the year and regularly thereafter will help avoid some of these problems. For example, inform parents about the homework policies for your classroom, which may include:

- What types of activities will be assigned?
- How often will homework be assigned?
- How much time will a typical homework assignment take to complete?
- How much and what type of help should parents give?
- What if parents have questions about a homework assignment?
- How do students make up work when they're absent?

Also, be sure to provide some advice to parents about providing a positive homework environment in the home, such as:

- Find a place in your home where materials are available (books, paper, pencil, lighting) and distractions are minimal (a quiet spot to read and write). Keep in mind that boys and girls can be quite different in how and where they like to do their homework. Boys especially may find it more productive to stand up at the kitchen counter or lie down on the living room floor while they work. The bottom line here is: are they getting the work done? Help parents understand that each child's individual needs will differ.

- Establish a schedule and routine for homework so you and your student know what to expect. Try not to require your child to complete homework the minute he or she gets home from school. A "brain break" that allows for movement, a nutritious snack, and some free expression will help prepare your child to focus on homework a little later! Try to schedule at least some of the homework time when you are available for questions and assistance. This also provides opportunities to discuss your student's work.

- If necessary, set a timer so that students can learn how they are using their time and to challenge them to work with greater focus.

Parents should also know your expectations for their involvement in the children's homework. Following are some guidelines that might be helpful in this regard:

- Your student should take the lead in scheduling and doing homework. Your role is to provide support and guidance as needed.

- Show interest in homework activities on a regular basis so you're not involved only if there are problems.

- Acknowledge progress in completing activities and in the learning that is going on.

- When providing help, ask how the class typically approaches an activity and follow the routines that your child is familiar with.

- Help your child seek additional resources as needed (such as helping to locate materials on a specific topic, or find someone who can help with an activity if you are not familiar with the content).

Some teachers design homework activities that require families to become involved in the activity itself. *The National Network of Partnership Schools* (www.csos.jhu.edu/p2000/) has developed a process called Teachers Involve Parents in Schoolwork (TIPS) Interactive Homework.

Interactive homework assignments require students to talk with someone at home about a question, issue, or project that is connected to what students are learning in class. Often, these activities move beyond having students ask for help with an activity and get family members involved in contributing to the activity. In this way, families are discussing subject matter with students and finding out more about what they are learning in school.

You can access www.csos.jhu.edu/p2000/tips/TIPSmain.htm for more information about TIPS interactive homework, sample activities, and blank TIPS templates.

Here are a few examples of the types of TIPS activities you will find:

- Students are asked to interview a family member about a topic.

- Students are asked to survey family members of a certain age group about a topic.

- Students are asked to write a draft of a story, share it with a family member, and ask the family member for more examples related to their topic.

- Students are asked to find examples of objects at home related to a topic being studied, such as products that come from animals. Or they may be asked to document whether/how families participate in activities such as recycling.

Besides helping parents understand how homework fits into your classroom plan, make sure you are keeping up with current research on homework, and ask yourself these questions:

- How is the homework assigned relevant to the learning objectives?

- Am I evaluating homework based on quantity or quality?

- Am I offering students choices of homework assignments, giving then a chance to incorporate their strengths and interests?

- How much weight does homework carry in assigning grades and who benefits or suffers under the current system?

Find time in your already busy schedule to review current research on homework. It's something you can do that can have a significant impact on your students' attitudes and grade—and a profound affect on the performance of your boys.

If you have parents who are struggling with their child's homework issues, point them in the direction of a good book on the topic. You might also find these books helpful to read yourself:

Ending the Homework Hassle: Understanding, Preventing and Solving School Performance Problems by John Rosemond (Canter Associates, 1987)

Homework Without Tears: A Parent's Guide for Motivating Children to Do Homework and to Succeed in School by Lee Cander and Lee Hausner (Andrews McNeel, 1990)

"Smart Boys, Bad Grades"

A report by Julie Coates and William Draves, 2006

Available at www.smartboysbadgrades.com/smartboys_badgrades.pdf

This well-researched report addresses the difference in how boys and girls approach and complete homework and the affect that difference has on grades. The Web site offers tips for parents and teachers, in addition to sharing the complete report.

According to Coates and Draves: "If you look at boys' work, their test scores are fairly equal with girls. It is homework where boys overall fall well short of girls. . . . We also confirmed this with interviews with dozens of boys. We also did a random survey of 200 K–12 teachers across North America. Some 84 percent said boys turn in homework late, only 4 percent said girls. Another 8 percent said neither, and the final 4 percent said they did not know. A second question asked whether turning homework in on time would improve the students' homework scores. Some 96 percent said yes, only 4 percent said no. Thus, K–12 teachers confirm that boys turn in homework late more than girls, and that boys are penalized for turning in homework late."

(Used with permission)

Additionally, the National Education Association has a helpful online article titled, "Help Your Child Get the Most Out of Homework." It is available at www.nea.org/parents/homework.html.

We must, indeed, all hang together or, most assuredly, we shall all hang separately.

—Benjamin Franklin

Practical Ideas for Your Classroom

➡ Create a school climate and structures that support family involvement.

➡ Provide families with a list of required mastery skills for each subject taught at your grade level.

➡ Help create a parent resource center in your school. Provide materials on issues of concern to parents, such as child development, health and safety, drug education, special education, and so on. Include information about local parenting and social services agencies. If possible, provide sample textbooks, extension activities, software, and audio and videotapes.

➡ Create a classroom Web site and include a parent page.

➡ Set up a "homework hotline" that students or parents can call to get forgotten or missed assignments.

➡ Invite parents to present talks or demonstrations about their specialized knowledge or skills.

➡ Maintain regular communication by sending home weekly folders of student work, monthly calendars of special events to be celebrated or taught, and a regular class newsletter.

➡ Compile a wish list that includes both goods (from craft sticks to carpet squares to software) and services (from stapling newsletters to chaperoning field trips to coordinating special events) that parents might provide. Be sure the list includes many free or inexpensive items and activities that do not demand a great deal of time or a long-term commitment.

➡ Practice an open-door, open-mind policy. Teachers can invite parents to visit the class at any time that is convenient for the parent. When they visit, parents can monitor their child's perceptions of a situation and see for themselves what the teacher is trying to achieve with his or her students.

➡ Let parents know how they can be helpful and solicit their assistance with specific activities. The more involved parents are in what goes on in the classroom, the more likely they are to understand the teacher's goals and practices.

➡ Accommodate parents' schedules to the greatest degree possible when scheduling conferences and special events.

➡ Students can become your best recruiters for your conferences. They can
   ➡ Create handwritten invitations to parents
   ➡ Remind parents of the upcoming event
   ➡ Help plan which work samples parents will discuss during the event

➡ Invite parents to visit classrooms whenever they wish to do so and send special invitations for culmination of a unit, puppet play, songfest, and so on.

➡ Schedule a parent-teacher conference in a student's home.

➡ Organize a special effort to contact hard-to-reach parents through telephone calls, home visits, and special mailed invitations to parents in home languages.

➡ Invite fathers to school to serve as a guest speaker, read one-on-one with a student, or share books that they love.

➡ Take note of the fact that more fathers are participating in school activities, and be sure to include fathers in all school communications.

➡ Have children prepare a luncheon for parents, teachers, and themselves. Send handwritten invitations.

➡ Invite each parent to have lunch with his or her child at school during American Education Week.

➡ Hold a bean-and-hot-dog supper and open house coordinated with a talent show. Allow children to show their parents around the school building.

➡ Hold a Grandparents' Day to honor grandparents and other special seniors with recognition given to those who've made a contribution to the school.

➡ Make at least one positive phone call per week to a parent to report on a child's accomplishment.

➡ Send home an overview of weekly lesson plans.

➡ Have parents fill out a survey at the beginning of the year to tell you about their child.

➡ Send a survey after parent-teacher conferences. Ask how effective the conference was and what additional kinds of information parents want to receive about your classroom.

➡ Follow up on problems and resolve complaints—no matter how small or insignificant they may seem. Little things have a way of building into big things.

➡ If you are requesting the conference in response to a specific problem with the child, allow some time to cool off before meeting with the parent. You'll be less emotionally charged and more objective after a couple of days.

➧ Communicate early and often if a child is struggling in any area.

Check out these additional resources:

➧ **Project Appleseed** (www.projectappleseed.org)
This non-profit, national campaign advocates improvement in public schools by increasing parental involvement in U.S. schools.

➧ **The National PTA** (www.pta.org)
This site provides a number of documents offering ideas for teachers and schools who want to encourage and promote parental involvement in education.

➧ **National Network of Partnership Schools** (www.csos.jhu.edu/P2000/)
Established by researchers at Johns Hopkins University, this organization helps schools, districts, and states develop and maintain programs that promote school-family-community partnerships.

WRAPPING UP THE MAIN POINTS

• Parental involvement in their child's education is one of the greatest predictors of the child's success in school, including better grades and lower retention and suspension rates.

• Successful communication with parents involves understanding the purpose and the goal of the communication, in addition to making sure you understand the audience and the best approach to take. Plan ahead for conferences.

• It is especially important to welcome parents who don't feel comfortable in the school setting. Make extra outreach efforts to families who may not feel included in the school community for any reason.

• Make an effort to get to know the student and his or her family through surveys, home visits, student sharing, and conferences.

• Harness technology to make communication easier and more effective. There are a number of online tools to help both you and parents stay up-to-date.

• Be proactive in discussing homework expectations, strategies, and the parents' role. Homework can support students' achievement and develop responsibility, as long as it doesn't become a wedge between the home and the school.

It takes two to speak *the truth—one to* speak, *and another to* hear.

—Henry David Thoreau

Epilogue

T HE sense of urgency is palpable. We feel it as we travel across the country working with teachers, parents and administrators. In an era of high-stakes testing, bulging curriculums, and shrinking resources, the fire that many educators once had for teaching is growing dimmer. We see this happening among our children as well. For too many children, the innate hunger for learning with which they came into this world is lost and they are drifting without purpose or joy. It's time to reclaim the joy and rekindle the fires—this is the sense of urgency we feel from teachers like you across the nation.

As we do presentations for teachers, we hear you saying, "This is just what we've been needing!" at every stop on our journey. The momentum is building as we link arms with you in a giant network of child advocates who are saying, "Wait a minute—what are we doing to our children here?" and "How is it that we have moved so far from what we know is best for kids?" Together, we must reexamine, rethink, and restructure schools one classroom at a time—and we have no time to waste. Every child whose core personality is not nurtured and whose unique needs are not met is one more child whose potential is unnecessarily limited or unrealized. We cannot lose any time in rediscovering the joys of teaching and learning— the human costs are simply too high.

With this book, we have endeavored to provide exactly what we've heard you requesting. We hope that our blend of cutting-edge brain science and the extensive and practical information about classroom strategies has helped you weave together the art and science of teaching. We also hope that you have marveled at the wonders of the human brain (as we do!) and have identified many new strategies to implement right away in your classroom. We also wonder whether you recognized some of the strategies and activities in this book as things you are already doing. We hope so! Teachers have tremendous experiential knowledge about what works with kids. We challenge you, then, to think more deeply about your current teaching practice—what you do, how you do it and why you do it—so that you can be more intentional and more informed in your instructional decision making.

Ultimately, we hope that all of you have developed a profound respect for the unique qualities that all students, both male and female, bring to the classroom. With this book, we've endeavored to open up a whole new way of thinking about your students and your classroom. May you be inspired and empowered to create a classroom culture that allows all children to experience true honoring, success, respect, and personal regard. When we look at our students and see opportunities rather than obstacles, we are limitless in our capacity to make the world a better place.

This is the source of our energy and passion. This is the urgency we feel from you to do the right work. It is the basis for the groundswell of support for reconnecting teaching with the nature of the learner. One child and one teacher at a time, we can not only rekindle the flame of learning—we can build a bonfire.

Sources

Chapter One

Baron-Cohen, S. (2003). *The essential difference: The truth about the male and female brain.* New York: Basic Books.

Blum, D. (1998). *Sex on the brain: The biological differences between men and women.* New York: Penguin Books.

Carter, R. (1998). *Mapping the mind.* Berkeley: University of California Press.

Jensen, E. (2000). *Brain-based learning: The new science of teaching and learning.* (Rev. ed.) San Diego, CA: Brain Store.

Jensen, E. (2006). *Enriching the brain: How to maximize every learner's potential.* San Francisco: Jossey-Bass.

Karges-Bone, L. (1998). *More than pink and blue: how gender can shape your curriculum.* Carthage, IL: Teaching and Learning Company.

Moir, A., & Jessel, D. (1992). *Brain sex: The real difference between men and women.* New York: Delta.

Rhoads, S. E. (2004). *Taking sex differences seriously.* San Francisco: Encounter Books.

Salomone, R. C. (2003). *Same, different, equal: Rethinking single-sex schooling.* New Haven, CT: Yale University Press.

Sousa, D. A. (2001). *How the brain learns.* (2nd ed.) Thousand Oaks, CA: Corwin Press.

Wolfe, P. (2001). *Brain matters: Translating research into classroom practice.* Alexandria, VA: Association for Supervision and Curriculum Development.

Chapter Two

Evanski, J. (2004). *Classroom activators.* San Diego: The Brain Store.

Gurian, M. (2002). *Boys and girls learn differently!: A guide for teachers and parents.* San Francisco: Jossey-Bass.

Gurian, M., & Stevens, K. (2004, November). With boys and girls in mind. *Educational Leadership, 62*(3), 21–26.

Gurian, M., & Stevens, K. (2005). *Minds of boys.* San Francisco: Jossey-Bass.

Jensen, E. (2000). *Learning with the body in mind.* Thousand Oaks, CA: Corwin Press.

Jensen, E. (2001). *Teaching with the arts in mind.* Alexandria, VA: ASCD.

King, K., & Gurian, M. (2006, October). Teaching to the minds of boys. *Educational Leadership.*

Sprenger, M. (1999). *Learning and memory: The brain in action.* Alexandria, VA: ASCD.

Summerford, C. (2005). *Action-packed Classrooms: Movement Strategies to Invigorate K–5 Learners.* San Diego: The Brain Store.

Chapter Three

Gould, R., Duey, K., & Epstein, E. (2000). *The time soldiers series.* Big Guy Books.

Gurian, M. (2002). *Boys and girls learn differently!: A guide for teachers and parents.* San Francisco, Jossey-Bass.

Gurian, M., & Stevens, K. (2004, November). With boys and girls in mind. *Educational Leadership, 62*(3), 21–26.

Gurian, M., & Stevens, K. (2005). *Minds of boys.* San Francisco: Jossey-Bass.

Hawkins, J. (2006, October). Think before you write. *Educational Leadership.* 63–66.

Helmstetter, S. (1995). *What is self-talk. The Self-Talk Solution.* Retrieved from www.selftalk.com/index.html

King, K., & Gurian, M. (2006, October). Teaching to the minds of boys. *Educational Leadership.*

Porter, K., & Foster, J. (1990). *Visual athletics.* Dubuque, IA: Wm. C. Publishers.

Sprenger, M. (1999). *Learning and memory: The brain in action.* Alexandria, VA: ASCD.

Strete, C. K. (1999). *The lost boy and the monster.* New York: Putnam Juvenile.

Chapter Four

Canadian adolescent boys and literacy. (2003) Retrieved from www.education.ualberta.ca/boysandliteracy/

Colorado Department of Education. (1999). *Unit of student assessment.* Retrieved from www.cde.state.co.us

Dodson, S. (1998). *100 books for girls to grow on.* New York: Harper Paperbacks.

Durica, K. (2004). *An unleveled playing field: The ways in which school culture undermines and undervalues boys' writing.* The Colorado Reading Council Journal.

Fletcher, R. (2006). *Boy writers: Reclaiming their voices.* Portland, ME: Stenhouse.

Gurian, M. (2000). *What stories does my son need?: a guide to books and movies that build character in boys.* Los Angeles: Tarcher.

King, K., & Gurian, M. (2006, October). Teaching to the minds of boys. *Educational Leadership.*

Morpurgo, M. (2000). *The Kingfisher book of great boy stories: A treasury of classics from children's literature.* Kingfisher.

Newkirk, T. (2002). *Misreading masculinity: Boys, literacy, and popular culture.* Portsmouth, NH: Heinemann.

O'Dean, K. (1997). *Great books for girls: More than 600 books to inspire today's girls and tomorrow's women.* New York: Ballantine.

O'Dean, K. (1998). *Great books for boys: More than 600 books for boys, 2 to 14.* New York: Ballantine.

Peterson, S. (2000). Fourth, sixth, and eighth graders' preferred writing topics and identification of gender markers in stories. *The Elementary School Journal, 101*(1), 79–100.

Sandberg, R. (1999). *The Kingfisher book of great girls stories: a treasury of classics from children's literature.* Kingfisher.

Scieszka, J. (2005). *Guys write for guys read.* New York: Viking Juvenile.

Smith, M. W., & Wilhelm, J. (2002). *Reading don't fix no Chevys: literacy in the lives of young men.* Portsmouth, NH: Heinemann.

Vitali, F. *Descriptive character analysis.* Retrieved from www.col-ed.org/cur/lang/lang17.txt

Welden, A. (1998). *Girls that rocked the world: Heroines from Sacagawea to Sheryl Swoopes.* Beyond Words Publishing.

Chapter Five

Applebee, A. N. (1996). *Curriculum as conversation.* Chicago: University of Chicago Press.

Dee, Z. *Team building.* Retrieved from www.sonoma.edu/kinesiology/ppep/experts/team.htm

Department of Geosciences at Oregon State University. *Volcano world. A collaborative higher education, K–12, and public outreach project of the North Dakota and Oregon space grant consortia.* Retrieved from http://volcano.und.edu/vwdocs/msh/llc/is/cl.html

Harvey, D. (2002). *What are literature circles?* Retrieved from www.literaturecircles.com/article1.htm

Kennesaw State University. (2006). *Kennesaw State University educational technology training center.* Retrieved from http://edtech.kennesaw.edu/intech/cooperativelearning.htm#elements

Kihn, L. *Establish a positive community atmosphere in your classroom through team-building activities.* Teachers Network: Who We Are. Retrieved from www.teachersnetwork.org/ntol/howto/start/teambuild.htm

McLaughlin, M. W., & Talbert, J. E. (2001). *Professional communities and the work of high school teaching.* Chicago: University of Chicago Press.

Schick, B. *Classroom interpreters—interpreters and children—cognitive/social development and educational interpreting.* Retrieved from www.classroominterpreting.org/Interpreters/children/Cognitive/index.asp

Schlick, N., Katherine, L., & Johnson, N. J. (1999). *Getting started with literature circles.* Christopher-Gordon Publishers.

Wilhelm, J. (2002). *Action strategies for deepening comprehension.* New York: Scholastic

Chapter Six

Balkcom, S. (1992, June). *Office of research education consumer guide, 1.* Retrieved from www.ed.gov/pubs/OR/ConsumerGuides/cooplear.html

Canadian adolescent boys and literacy. (2003) Retrieved from www.education.ualberta.ca/boysandliteracy/

Deci, E. L., Koestner, R., & Ryan, R. M. (2001). Extrinsic rewards and intrinsic motivation in education: Reconsidered once again. *Review of Educational Research, 71,* 1–27.

Deci, E. L., & Ryan, R. M. (2002). The paradox of achievement: The harder you push, the worse it gets. Improving academic achievement. *Contributions of Social Psychology 59–85.* New York: Academic Press.

Diamond, M., & Hopson, J. (1998). *Magic trees of the mind.* New York: Penguin Group.

diSessa. A. (1998). *Changing minds.* Cambridge: MIT Press.

Dunton, S. (2006). Building a microsociety. *Educational Leadership.* 56–60.

Forbus, K. (1997, May/June). Using qualitative physics to create articulate educational software. *IEEE Expert,* 32–41.

Gurian, M. (2002). *Boys and girls learn differently!: A guide for teachers and parents.* San Francisco: Jossey-Bass.

Gurian, M., & Stevens, K. (2004, November). With boys and girls in mind. *Educational Leadership, 62*(3), 21–26.

Gurian, M., & Stevens, K. (2005). *Minds of boys.* San Francisco: Jossey-Bass.

Hopkins, G. (2004, August). *Simulations engage students in active learning.* Retrieved from www.education-world.com/a_curr/curr391.shtml

Global School Net. (2000). *Introduction to Networked Project-Based Learning.* Retrieved from www.gsn.org/web/pbl/whatis.htm

Jobs for the Future. (1983). *Creating strategies for educational and economic opportunity.* Retrieved from www.jff.org/

King, K., & Gurian, M. (2006, October). Teaching to the minds of boys. *Educational Leadership.*

Lent, R. (2006, October). In the company of critical thinkers. *Educational Leadership,* 68–72.

McKenzie, J. (2005). *Learning to question, to wonder, to learn.* FNO Press.

Miller, A. (1991). Personality types, learning styles and educational goals. *Educational Psychology, 11*(3–4), 217–238.

National Research Council Committee on Increasing High School Students' Engagement and Motivation to Learn. (2004). *Engaging schools: Fostering high school motivation to learn.* Washington DC: National Academies Press.

Scherer, M. (2006, September). Celebrate strengths, nurture affinities: A conversation with Mel Levine. *Educational Leadership,* 8–15.

Smith, M. W., & Wilhelm, J. (2002). *Reading don't fix no Chevys: Literacy in the lives of young men.* Portsmouth, NH: Heinemann.

Squire, K., Barnett, M., Grant, J. M., & Higginbotham, T. *Electromagnetism supercharged! Learning physics with digital simulation games.* Madison, WI: Curriculum & Instruction, School of Education, University of Wisconsin-Madison. Retrieved from www.educationarcade.org/files/articles/Supercharged/SuperchargedResearch.pdf

Steinberg, A. (1998). *Dimensions of quality project-based learning.* Retrieved from http://www.essentialschools.org/cs/resources/view/ces_res/85

Vince, G. (2004, February). Teen brains show low motivation. Retrieved from www.NewScientist.com

Wilhelm, J. (2002). *Action strategies for deepening comprehension.* New York: Scholastic

Chapter Seven

Alexander, M., & Beatty, L. (1996, May). Music improves emotional awareness [letter]. *Family Medicine, 28*(5), 318.

Allen, R. H. (2001). *Impact teaching: Ideas and strategies for teachers to maximize student learning.* Boston: Allyn & Bacon.

Blakey, E., & Spence, S. (1990). Developing metacognition. *ERIC Digest.* Retrieved July 2002, from www.ed.gov/databases/ERIC_Digests/ed327218.html

Chicken lips and lizard hips. On *For our children.* (1999). Kid Rhino.

Gurian, M. (2002). *Boys and girls learn differently!: A guide for teachers and parents.* San Francisco: Jossey-Bass.

Gurian, M., & Stevens, K. (2005). *Minds of boys.* San Francisco: Jossey-Bass.

Harth, E. (1999, June/July). The emergence of art and language in the human brain: Art and the brain. *Journal of Consciousness Studies. 6*(6–7), 97–115.

Hill, B. C., & Ruptic, C. (1994). *Practical aspects of authentic assessment: Putting the pieces together.* 206–7. Norwood, MA: Christopher-Gordon.

Jensen, E. (2000). *Learning with the body in mind.* Thousand Oaks, CA: Corwin Press.

Jensen, E. (2001). *Teaching with the arts in mind.* Alexandria, VA: ASCD.

Ramachandran, V. S., & Hirstein, W. (1999, June/July). The science of art: Art and the brain. *Journal of Consciousness Studies, 6*(6–7), 15–51.

Science Daily. (1995). *Social exclusion changes brain function and can lead to poor decision-making.* Retrieved from www.sciencedaily.com/releases/ 2006/11/061108154256.htm

Chapter Eight

Blacher, J., & Eisenhower, A. (2006). Better than teacher's pet: Building relationships with teachers in the early school years. *Exceptional Parent Magazine.*

Brooks, R. (2000, September). *Education and "charismatic" adults: To touch a student's heart and mind.* Retrieved from www.drrobertbrooks.com

Brooks, R. *The educator's mindset: The basis for touching a student's mind and heart.* Retrieved from www.drrobertbrooks.com

Brooks, R. *The self-esteem teacher.* Retrieved from www.drrobertbrooks.com

Bryk, A. S., & Schneider B. (2002). *Trust in schools: A core resource for improvement.* New York: The Russell Safe Foundation.

Burke, D. L. (1996). Multi-year teacher/student relationships are a long-overdue arrangement. *Phi Delta Kappan, 77*(5), 360–361. (No. EJ 516 053)

Checkley, K. (1995). Multiyear education: Reaping the benefits of "looping."*ASCD Education Update, 37*(8), 1–6.

Craig, R. P. (1996). Student-teacher relationship: A Buddhist perspective. *Clearinghouse, 69*(5), 285–286.

Grant, J., & Johnson, B. (1995). Looping, the two grade cycle: A good starting place. *A Common Sense Guide to Multiage Practices, Primary Level.* 33–36. Columbus, OH: Teacher's Publishing Group.

Gurian, M. (1998). *Fine young man: What parents, mentors and educators can do to shape adolescent boys into exceptional men.* New York: Tarcher.

Hanson, B. (1995). Getting to know you—multiyear teaching. *Educational Leadership, 53*(3), 42–43. (No. EJ 514 699).

Henricsson, L., & Rydell, A. (2004, April). *Elementary school children with behavior problems: Teacher-child relations and self-perception: A prospective study. Merrill-Palmer Quarterly.*

Lincoln, R. (1997). Multi-year instruction: Establishing student-teacher relationships. *Schools in the Middle, 6*(3), 50–52. (No. EJ 538 167)

Mostert, M. P. (1998). *Interprofessional collaboration in schools.* Boston: Allyn and Bacon.

National School Public Relations Association. (1995, September). *Problem parents buy into multi-year relationships.* It Starts on the Frontline, 1.

Noddings, N. (1992). *The challenge to care in schools: An alternative approach to education.* New York: Teachers College Press.

Osterman, K. (2000). Students' need for belonging in the school community. *Review of Educational Research, 70*(3), 323–367.

Pianta, R. C. (1999). *Enhancing relationships between children and teachers.* Washington, DC: American Psychological Association.

Pianta, R. C., & Walsh D. J. (1996). *High-Risk Children in Schools: Constructing Sustaining Relationships.* New York: Routledge.

Pianta, R. C., Hamre, B., & Stuhlman, M. (in press). *Relationships between teachers and children: Comprehensive handbook of psychology, 7.* Educational Psychology. New York: Wiley.

Pianta, R. C., La Paro, K., Cox, M., Payne, C., & Bradley, R. (2002). The relation of kindergarten classroom environment to teacher, family, and school characteristics and child outcomes. *The Elementary School Journal, 102,* 225–238.

Pianta, R. C., Steinberg, M., & Rollins, K. (1995). The first two years of school: Teacher-child relationships and deflections in children's classroom adjustment. *Development and Psychopathology, 7,* 295–312.

Saft, E. W., & Pianta, R. C. (2001). Teachers'perceptions of their relationships with students: Effects of child age, gender, and . . .—group of 6. *School Psychology Quarterly.*

Seligman, A. B. (1997). *The problem of trust.* Princeton, NJ: Princeton University Press.

Shepro, T. (1995). The teacher factor. *American School Board Journal, 182*(6), 43. (No. EJ 506 516)

Stipek, D. (2006). Relationships matter. *Educational Leadership, 64*(1), 46–49.

Yoon, J. S. (2002). Teacher characteristics as predictors of teacher-student relationships: Stress, negative affect, and self-efficacy. *Social Behavior and Personality.*

Chapter Nine

American Academy of Pediatrics, Committee on Public Education. (2001, November). Media violence. *Pediatrics, 108*(5), 1222–1226.

Baker, J. A., Terry, T., Bridger, R., & Winsor, A. (1997). Schools as Caring Communities: A Relational Approach to School Reform. *School Psychology Review.*

Battistich, V., Solomon, D., Watson, M., & Schaps, E. (1997). Caring School Communities. *Educational Psychologist, 32*(3), 137–151.

Bedley, Gene. (2000, August). Payoffs and benefits of character development. *National Character Education Center.* Retrieved from www.ethicsusa.com/

Benninga, J. S., Berkowitz, M. W., Kuehn, P., & Smith, K. (2003). The relationship of character education implementation and academic achievement in elementary schools. *Journal of Research in Character Education, 1*(1), 19–32.

Berkowitz, M. W., & Bier, M. C. (2005). *What works?* Washington, DC: Character Education Partnership.

Beverly, B. (2001). *Complete no bullying program curriculum: Preventing bullying at school: Complete curriculum.* Hazelden/Johnson Institute.

Bridwell, N. (1980). *Clifford goes to Hollywood.* Scholastic.

Canto, J. (1998). *Mommy, I'm scared: How TV and movies frighten children and what we can do to protect them.* San Diego: Harcourt Brace.

Center for the Advancement of Ethics and Character (CAEC) at Boston University. (1989). Retrieved from www.bu.edu/education/caec/index.html

Character Education Partnership. (2005). Retrieved from www.character.org

DePaola, T. (1980). *Now one foot, now the other.* New York: Putnam.

Federman, J. (1998). *National television violence study, 3.* Thousand Oaks, CA: Sage.

Feehan, M., McGee, R., Williams, S. M., & Nada-kRaja, S. (1995, May). Models of adolescent psychopathology: Childhood risk and the transition to adulthood. *Journal of the American Academy of Child and Adolescent Psychiatry, 34*(5), 670–679.

Garrity, C., Jens, K., Porter, W., Sager, N., & Short-Camilli, C. (2000). *Bully-proofing your school: A comprehensive approach for elementary schools.* Sopris West.

Ginott, H. (1975). *Teacher and child: A book for parents and teachers,* (2nd Ed.) New York: Avon Books.

Goleman, D. (2006). *Emotional intelligence: Why it can matter more than IQ.* (10th anniversary edition). New York: Bantam.

Hancox R. J., Milne B. J., & Poulton R. (2005, July). Association of television viewing during childhood with poor educational achievement. *Arch Pediatr Adolesc Med. 159*(7). 614–618.

Huitt, W. (1988). Personality differences between Navajo and non-Indian college students: Implications for instruction. *Equity & Excellence, 24*(1), 71–74. Retrieved May, 1999, from http://chiron.valdosta.edu/whutt/papers/mbtinav.html

Huitt, W. (2005, January). Lesson plans that connect academic instruction and character education. *Educational Psychology Interactive.* Valdosta, GA: Valdosta State University. Retrieved from http://chiron.valdosta.edu/whuitt/brilstar/Character/chared_index.html

Johnson J. G., Cohen P., Smailes E. M., Kasen S., & Brook J. S. (2002, March) Television viewing and aggressive behavior during adolescence and adulthood. *Science, 29; 295*(5564), 2468–2471.

Kane, R. (1985). *Free will and values.* Albany: State University of New York Press.

Lama, D., & Cutler, H. C. (1998). *The art of happiness: A handbook for living.* Riverhead Hardcover.

Lickona, T. (1992). *Educating for character.* New York: Bantam.

Lickona, T., Schaps, E., & Lewis, C. (2005). *11 characteristics of effective character education.* The Character Education Partnership.

Lucks, A. (1988, October). Helper's high: Volunteering makes people feel good, physically and emotionally. *Psychology Today.* Retrieved from www.findarticles.com/p/articles/mi_m1175/is_n10_v22/ai_6652854

Maryland State Department of Education. (2003). *MSDE Fact Sheet.* Retrieved from www.mcps.k12.md.us/curriculum/charactered/md/factsheet.shtm

Mischel, W. (1996). *From good intentions to willpower: The psychology of action.* 197–218. New York: Guilford Press.

New Horizons for Learning. (2006, August). *Character education.* Retrieved from www.newhorizons.org

Senate Committee on the Judiciary. (1999, September). *Children, violence, and the media: a report for parents and policy makers.* Retrieved June 14, 2006, from http://judiciary.senate.gov/oldsite/mediavio.htm

Soto, G. (1992). *Too many tamales.* New York: Putnam & Grossett.

Tallon, A. (1997). *Head and heart: Affection, cognition, volition as triune consciousness.* New York: Fordham University.

University of Michigan Health System. (2006). What do I need to know about children and television. *Your Child.* Retrieved from www.med.umich .edu/1libr/yourchild/tv.htm#violence

Utah State Office of Education. *Character education.* Retrieved from www.usoe .k12.ut.us/curr/char_ed/

Walberg, H., & Wynne, E. (1989). *Character education: Toward a preliminary consensus. Moral development and character education: A dialogue,* 19–36. Berkley, CA: McCutchan.

Weissbourd, R. (2003). Moral Teachers, Moral Students. *Educational Leadership, 60*(6), 6–11.

Werner, E. (1990). *Protective factors and individual resilience. Handbook of early childhood intervention.* Cambridge, England: Cambridge University Press.

Yokota, F., & Thompson, K. M. (2000, May). Violence in G-rated animated films. *JAMA.* 24–31; *283*(20), 2716–2720.

Chapter Ten

Bauch, J. P. (2000). *Parent involvement partnerships with technology.* Nashville, TN: Transparent School Model.

Bloom, L. R. (2001). I'm poor, I'm single, I'm a mom and deserve respect: Advocating schools as and with mothers in poverty. *Educational Studies, 32,* 30–316.

Building Community Partnerships for Learning. Based on *Strong Families, Strong Schools,* by Ballen, J., & Moles, O. for the National Family Initiative of the U.S. Department of Education. (1994, September). Retrieved from www .projectappleseed.org/strongfamiliesschools.pdf

Carey, N., Lewis, L., & Farris, E. (1998). *Parent involvement in children's education: Efforts by public elementary schools.* Washington, DC: U.S. Department of Education Office of Educational Research and Improvement. Retrieved from nces.ed.gov/pubs98/98032.pdf

Christenson, S. L., & Sheridan, S. M. (2001). *Schools and families: Creating essential connections for learning.* New York: Guildford Press.

Christenson, S. *Parent-Teacher Partnerships: Creating Essential Connections for Children's Reading and Learning.* Harvard Family Research Project. Retrieved June 14, 2004, from www.gse.harvard.edu/hfrp/projects/fine/resources/ materials/reading_success_workshop.html

Coates, J., & Draves, W. A. (2006). *Smart boys, bad grades.* The Learning Resources Network.

Comer, J., Haynes, N., Joyner, E., & Ben-Avie, M. (Eds.). (1996). *Rallying the whole village: The Comer process for reforming education.* New York: Teachers College Press.

DeMoss, S., & Vaughn, C. (1999). A parent cultures perceptions of parent involvement. *School Community Journal, 9,* 67–83.

Drake, D. D. (2000). Parents and families as partners in the education process: Collaboration for the success of students in public schools. *ERS Spectrum, 18*(2), 34–39.

Elam, S. M., Lowell, C. R., & Gallup, A. M. (1994, September). The 26th Annual Phi Delta Kappa/Gallup Poll of the Public's Attitudes Toward the Public Schools. *Phi Delta Kappan.*

Elman, R. (1999). The relationship among school-home communication. Parent and teacher attitudes and teacher's practices with parent involvement. *Dissertation Abstracts International, 60*(07), 2367A. (UMI No. 9938903)

Epstein, J. (1996). Family/school/community partnerships: Caring for the children we share. *Phi Delta Kappan, 76,* 701–712.

Gutman, L. M. (2000). Parents management of their children's education within the home, at school, and in the community: An examination of African-American families living in poverty. *The Urban Review, 32,* 1–24.

Helling, M. K. (1996). School-home communication and parental expectations. *School Community Journal, 6,* 81–99.

Henderson, A., & Berla, N. (Eds.) (1994). *A new generation of evidence: The family is critical to student achievement.* National Committee for Citizens in Education.

Hoover-Dempsey, K., & Sandler, H. (1997). Why do parents become involved in their children's education. *Review of Educational Research, 67,* 3–42.

James, D. W., Jurich, S., & Estes, S. (2001). *Raising minority academic achievement: A compendium of education programs and practices.* Washington, DC: American Youth Policy Forum.

Kessler-Sklar, S. L., & Baker, A.J.L. (2000). School district parent involvement policies and programs. *The Elementary School Journal, 101,* 101–119.

Lupi, M. H., & Tong, V. M. (2001). Reflecting on personal interaction style to promote successful cross-cultural school-home partnerships. *Preventing School Failure, 45,* 162–166.

McDermott, P., & Rothenberg, J. (2000, October). Why Urban Parents Resist Involvement in their Children's Elementary Education. *The Qualitative Report, 5,* (3–4). Retrieved from www.nova.edu/ssss/QR/QR5-3/mcdermott.html

McKenzie, W. (2000, December). *Home-school communication, 3*(12). Retrieved from http://surfaquarium.com/newsletter/home.htm

McNamara, O., Hustler, D., Stronahc, I., Rodrigo, M., Beresford, E., & Botcherby, S. (2000). Room to maneuver: Mobilizing the active partner in home school relations. *British Educational Research Journal, 26,* 473–489.

National Center for Education Statistics. (1997, September). *Fathers' involvement in their children's schools.* Retrieved from http://nces.ed.gov/pubs98/fathers/

National Education Association. (2006). *Help your child get the most out of homework.* Retrieved from www.nea.org/parents/homework.html

National Network of Partnership Schools. (1996). *Teachers involve parents in schoolwork (TIPS) interactive homework.* Retrieved from www.csos.jhu.edu/p2000/

Rimm-Kauffman. (1999). Patterns of family-school contact in preschool and kindergarten. *School Psychology Review, 28,* 426–438.

Rosaen, C. *Tools for engaging communities. Assist beginning teachers.* Retrieved from http://assist.educ.msu.edu/ASSIST/classroom/community/indexcomm.htm

Scribner, J. D., Young, M. D., & Pedroza, A. (1999). *Building collaborative relationships with parents. Lessons from high-performing Hispanic schools: Creating learning communities.* New York; Teacher College Press.

Shartrand, A., Weiss, H., Kreider, H., & Lopez, E. (1997). *New skills for new schools: Teacher preparation in family involvement.* Washington, DC: U.S. Department of Education.

Weiss, H., Kreider, H., Levine, E., Mayer, E., Stadler, J., & Vaughan, P. (1998). *Beyond the Parent-Teacher Conference: Diverse Patterns of Home-School Communication. American Educational Research Association Annual Conference.* San Diego, California. Retrieved from www.gse.harvard.edu/hfrp/pubs/onlinepubs/beyondptc.html

Winters, W. G. (1993). *African American mothers and urban schools: The power of participation.* New York: Lexington Books.

Index